THE
OFF ROAD
AND
4 WHEEL DRIVE
H A N D B O O K

This book is dedicated to Jodie,
the one person who keeps this author
from going too far off-road

THE OFF ROAD AND 4 WHEEL DRIVE HANDBOOK

Nigel Fryatt

MRP

MOTOR RACING PUBLICATIONS LTD
Unit 6, The Pilton Estate, 46 Pitlake,
Croydon CR0 3RY, England

ISBN 0 947981 26 8

First published 1988

Write for a free complete catalogue of MRP books to
Motor Racing Publications Ltd, Unit 6,
The Pilton Estate, 46 Pitlake, Croydon CR0 3RY

Photoset by Tek-Art Ltd, West Wickham, Kent

Printed in Great Britain by
Netherwood, Dalton & Co Ltd
Bradley Mills, Huddersfield, West Yorkshire

CONTENTS

ABOUT THE AUTHOR

Nigel Fryatt has been a motoring journalist for over 10 years. He became deeply involved in the 4x4 scene when appointed Editor of the monthly magazine *Off Road and 4 Wheel Drive*. He has driven a wide variety of four-wheel drives both in the UK and through Europe and was a member of the 1988 Camel Trophy team that drove Land Rovers through Sulawesi in Indonesia.

Nigel's professional background includes working on *Autocar, Your Car* and *Sporting Cars* and contributing to numerous other magazines at home and abroad. He is now the editor of *Cars and Car Conversions*.

ACKNOWLEDGEMENTS

The author is only a small ingredient in the production of a book. This is certainly the case with *The Off Road and 4 Wheel Drive Handbook*. The whole idea, indeed the driving force to write it, has come from the enthusiasm of the readers of the magazine *Off Road and 4 Wheel Drive*. My thanks go to everyone who has been reading the magazine, making my job as Editor all the more enjoyable and easier! I am grateful that I was able to persuade John Blunsden and Ray Hutton of Motor Racing Publications that it was a worthy project for their stable — you see, the enthusiasm for off-roading can be infectious.

Much of the information for the book has been derived from my work on *Off Road and 4 Wheel Drive* over the last three years and for that I must thank the magazine's publisher Terry Grimwood for his encouragement and Mike Hallett and Brian Hartley for their help and patience. Link House has been the source for the majority of the pictures in this book, the photographers in question being Norman Hodson, Roger Phillips, Tony Butler and David Darby — Norman deserves a special thank you as by far the majority of the pictures are his, many of them taken in the rain, the cold and always, it seems, in the mud.

Final thoughts go to a machine: How on earth did people write books before the word processor was invented — or are journalists just getting soft?

Nigel Fryatt
Wimbledon
1988

Evolution not revolution: 40 years of Land Rover development is illustrated by this group ranging from the Series I, left foreground, through the Series II and its lightweight military derivative to the latest One Ten County at the top of the hill on the left.

1

What's special about four-wheel drive?

Four-wheel drives are special. Of that, there is no doubt. It's a unique motoring experience, not some short-lived fashionable fad. We're not talking about go-faster GT hot hatchbacks or cars that say TURBO down the flanks in letters 2 feet high. The four-wheel drive movement is in favour of a different form of motoring for people who are fed up with ordinary cars. If you are a four-wheel driver then you belong to a great family of fellow enthusiasts. And that family is growing.

Some people have been enjoying the fun of four-wheel drive for a long time because the activity, as we know it today, can be traced back to the Second World War. They say that necessity is the mother of invention, and during any war you have absolute necessity. Those in charge of the American forces in Europe decided that a light utility general-purpose vehicle was needed and that four-wheel drive was the basic requirement. The story of how the famous US Jeep came to production is an epic in itself and one that shows how big business will always win in battles against the individual or smaller company, even if the latter has all the good ideas.

The Jeep, therefore, was the first mass-produced light utility four-wheel drive and its impact was to be far greater than anyone could have imagined at the time. This versatile design was destined to father a whole new range of four-wheel drive vehicles.

It is, perhaps, understandable why the Jeep should have been responsible for the growth of four-wheel drives in the United States, but less understandable how the trend should have developed here. It happened because of the frustrations of a land owner in Wales and the commercial demands of a country striving to rebuild itself immediately after the war.

As you would expect, there was an acute shortage of many materials,

Land Rover Ninety County Station Wagon in 1988 turbo diesel form: despite increasing competition, particularly from the Japanese manufacturers, Solihull's 4x4 remains the favourite of many.

notably steel, during this period. The Rover Company were initially refused permission to restart civilian car production because of the steel shortage, but later they were given the go-ahead for limited production. The two men very much in the front line of all Rover's plans were the Wilks brothers, Spencer and Maurice. With all the restrictions on

The Range Rover, introduced in 1970, transformed the image of the four-wheel drive vehicle and in the opinion of many enthusiasts remains unchallenged to this day.

production, the brothers began to think about building some sort of agricultural machine that would not need a large amount of steel for the body. But what should they build?

The scene now shifts to a farm at Anglesey, in North Wales, where Maurice had a problem. He needed a machine that could do a multitude of tasks and cross a variety of different terrains. After trying a large, bulky and extremely thirsty ex-WD half-track, he decided instead to buy one of the many Willys Jeeps that had been left behind by the Americans. It did the job, but it upset Maurice Wilks greatly. After all, why should it be necessary to buy a foreign vehicle to do the job when he had a car company that was looking for the opportunity to build vehicles, yet was being restricted through lack of materials? The answer was obvious; Rover should design and build a British 'Jeep'.

That, of course, is a highly simplified, romantic, precis of how the first Land-Rover (originally it was hyphenated) came to be designed. Actually, designed is rather too grand a word, as the first prototype was little more than a copy of the Jeep using Rover parts wherever possible. Even its designer, Gordon Bashford, admitted that it was very much like the Jeep at first; it had virtually the same dimensions, but with the body made out of aluminium for lightness, better corrosion protection and, of course, because they didn't have the steel. Back in 1947 the similarity between the first Land-Rover and the Jeep was almost embarrassing:

	Jeep	Land-Rover
Wheelbase:	80in	80in
Width:	62in	60in
Length:	133in	132in
Track:	48in	50in
Engine:	4-cylinder, 2.1-litre	4-cylinder, 1.6-litre
	60bhp at 3,600rpm	55bhp at 4,000rpm
Weight:	2,315lb	2,520lb

More than 40 years on, little has been done to change the image of the Land Rover, which remains a predominantly agricultural machine, albeit with a high-quality price. Is that a little unfair? Perhaps, but certainly Land Rover have continued to produce vehicles seemingly without taking notice of what is happening in the rest of the world. The four-wheel drive revolution has occurred almost *despite* the actions of the Solihull manufacturer. The British four-wheel drive fraternity is still solidly based on the rock that is Land Rover, but far more has happened over the last few years; notably the Japanese have become involved and a four-wheel drive phenomenon has begun.

Obviously, the large number of Land Rover enthusiasts and users make up an important segment of the four-wheel drive market in the UK. As Land Rover celebrate their 40th year, many of these enthusiasts will have you believe that there is only one four-wheel drive manufacturer in the world, let alone the UK. But in many respects the UK market is the least significant to Land Rover. It is ironic that a machine that originated from a desire by one man not to have to 'buy foreign' should have become such a resounding export success. Of all Land Rovers built since 1948, 75% have been exported, and a similar figure applies to the Range Rover, which of course has been with us for a much shorter time. So Land Rover have been busy exporting to many countries around the globe while other manufacturers have started to gain significant four-wheel drive sales in the UK.

Land Rover pride themselves in what they call 'evolution not revolution', which explains why the models today bear such a strong resemblance to the original design. The concept hasn't changed at all, and mechanically, the most important specification change has been from selectable to permanent four-wheel drive with a central diff lock. The original Series I was permanent, but when the Series II was introduced in 1958 the drive became selectable and this situation remained through the Series II, IIA and III. When the Range Rover was introduced in 1970, however, the 'evolution' went back to permanent four-wheel drive and there was something of a 'revolution' in the suspension. The Range Rover was not a cart-sprung machine, but had coil springs all round and a suspension set-up that allowed for a great deal

Range Rover, Mitsubishi Shogun, Toyota Landcruiser, Mercedes-Benz G-Wagen: widening choice for the UK off-road market.

Suzuki LJ80 first appeared in the UK in 1979: small, tough and competent, if not very powerful, it presaged important things to come.

of wheel travel. Add to that an extremely flexible and torquey V8 engine and more recently a turbo diesel option (albeit an Italian engine) and you have what remains today the king of all mass-produced four-wheel drives, despite 1988 being its 18th year.

The Range Rover was a revelation, and it was only a matter of time before the same suspension set-up was put on the Land Rover. It first appeared on the One Ten in 1983 (the words in the model title refer to the wheelbase in inches). A year later it was followed by the Ninety (surprisingly, perhaps, its wheelbase is 92.9in) and by mid-1985 all Series III production had ceased. Land Rover now had three basic models (with a wide variety of derivatives) and they each had coil-sprung suspension. Tough and extremely competent off-road, they really remain at the top of the mass-produced four-wheel drive tree, but with the cheapest version costing more than £11,000 (rising to £27,000 for the Range Rover Vogue) a huge gap developed in the market place for cheaper models which, although they might not perform as well in 'ultimate' off-road conditions, could still be fun, exciting *and* reasonably priced. Enter the Japanese.

Suzuki is a name still better known in the UK for two wheels rather than four, and when they introduced the diminutive LJ80 model in the UK in 1979 many established off-road enthusiasts muttered that you would probably be better off with a bike. With only 797cc under the

13

bonnet it was lacking in power, but it was tough and, thanks to its small size and because it was relatively light, it proved competent enough off-road. A number of LJ80s started to appear around the UK trials scene and do commendably well. Although they lacked any real performance and creature comforts, it was obvious that the LJ80 represented only stage one in the Japanese manufacturer's master plan, and a few years later Suzuki returned with the SJ410 — and, bang, four-wheel drive became fashionable.

Without a shadow of doubt, the Suzuki SJ is now established as the four-wheel drive cult car of the 1980s. No other single vehicle has tapped the demand for 'something different' quite like the SJ. Still with the basic qualities of the original LJ80, it now has a larger engine (970cc), many more creature comforts, better fuel economy, but perhaps much more importantly it looks so good; a cheeky, bright little vehicle that looks the part in the local supermarket car park, or down at the local pub, but with the underlying strength that it is also a good off-roader.

The little four-cylinder engine buzzes away vigorously to produce only 45bhp, but the lightness of the vehicle makes this sufficient. On the road, those used to a 'normal' car may be somewhat surprised by the bouncy nature of the suspension and the imprecise feeling from the steering, but

No other vehicle has played a greater part in the blossoming enthusiasm for four-wheel drive than the popular Suzuki SJ: this is an SJ410 from 1984.

Suzuki Santana is Spanish-built – hence not subject to the voluntary quota restrictions to Japanese imports in the UK – and shows off the bright colours and fancy stripes that have helped to keep demand growing.

that's all due to the compromise of making the little beast such a good performer on the rough. Twist those free-wheeling hubs into the lock position, switch to four-wheel drive and you can drive the SJ through some surprising places. But for many owners the appearance alone has been a sufficient attraction; these are the people who only occasionally take them off-road — if at all. The Suzuki has sold so well in the UK that it is second in popularity to the Land Rover, and the future for the Japanese company looks even brighter now that they are importing the Suzuki Santana as well.

The importance of the Santana is that it is built in Spain and so does not fall within the 'Gentleman's Agreement' under which the importation of Japanese vehicles into the UK is restricted. Mechanically, it is the same as the Japanese-built SJ except for a slightly softer suspension (which makes it even more bouncy on-road) but it does have a five-speed gearbox (a four-speed box is standard on the Japanese SJs). Fancy colours and side stripes have helped to keep the demand growing, and the Suzuki SJ has brought many more new people to the world of off-roading; for such a tiny machine, it has a big heart.

Pushing hard for that second place in UK sales have been Mitsubishi. Imported by the Colt Car Company, the Mitsubishi Shoguns have grown

Mitsubishi Shogun, imported by the Colt Car Company: growing in stature and winning over some former Range Rover owners.

in stature and offer an excellent range of top-class off-roaders. Critics of the Shogun say it is not as good as the Range Rover, but that it gets close is a massive compliment for the Japanese machine. Certainly people who have owned older Range Rovers now consider the Shogun when it comes to replacement time.

Shoguns are considerably larger than the Suzukis we have just described and so they complement the market. It is unlikely, for instance, that anyone should consider buying either the Shogun or the SJ; they are different animals rather than competitors. Like the Suzuki, however, the Shogun has the usual Japanese feature of selectable four-wheel drive. Available in short-wheelbase (SWB) or long-wheelbase (LWB) forms with engine options that include both petrol and turbo diesel, the UK Shogun range includes a model to suit a wide variety of tastes.

Off-road, Shoguns are competent if not kings. They lack ground clearance (the transfer box is so low that it has a skid plate to cover it, lowering ground clearance further). They have independent front suspension which obviously helps with useful wheel movement, but at

Isuzu Trooper: very versatile challenger to the Shogun, similarly available in short or (as here) long wheelbase.

the back it's the semi-elliptic leaf-spring set-up which can see the Shogun struggle in deep ruts. However, it is always a matter of compromise, and in the Shogun's case this *relative* lack of off-road ability is offset by its on-road features. It is extremely 'user friendly' to drive — light, easy controls, notably for the gearbox — and it is comfortable, well-equipped and very roomy (five adults can be carried comfortably in the LWB with two occasional or child seats in the luggage area increasing versatility). An ideal family car with that extra ability to go where so many family cars don't! There is, however, a reservation concerning the engines; both could do with a little more power, especially when the vehicle is loaded and cruising on the motorway. Mitsubishi have an automatic transmission although, surprisingly, it was only introduced with the turbo diesel. Sluggish at the best of times, a diesel coupled to an automatic gearbox is not a combination that any reasonably serious off-roader would want to contemplate.

For a few years, Mitsubishi seemed to have had it all their own way in the UK. As we have said, the Shogun is not really comparable with the Suzuki, nor should it be with the Daihatsu, Nissan and Toyota ranges which, as will be explained later, are all rather different. The Isuzu Trooper, however, is another story.

Isuzu are going directly for the market that Mitsubishi have made their own, yet it could have been so different. The Isuzu Trooper is a Japanese off-road machine that has been on sale around the world for a number of years. They have been successful years, too, and it was only a matter of

17

time before the Trooper would come here. Unfortunately, there were a number of problems before it arrived and the British importer went into liquidation before the Trooper had even gone on sale. Very much at the eleventh hour, however, International Motors (the British importers of the Subaru range) stepped in and took up the franchise. This gave the Isuzu Trooper a solid business backing and an already well-established dealer network around the UK, something that is always a problem with new models.

It would have been a pity if we had lost the Trooper because it is a very good machine. Mitsubishi, however, may feel differently as it is a direct competitor to the Shogun. Around the same size, the Trooper is also available in LWB and SWB body styles with a choice of turbo diesel or petrol engines. Ground clearance is slightly better that the Shogun's (9in compared to 8.1in) but, more importantly, the transfer box is well tucked up out of harm's way. Suspension is like the Shogun's with independent coil springs and wishbones at the front and semi-elliptic leaf springs at the

Daihatsu Fourtrack: bigger than a Suzuki but smaller than a Shogun or Trooper, with distinctive styling and a choice of wheelbase and power unit.

rear. It's a close-run thing, but in similar conditions with a similarly competent driver, the Trooper probably edges it over the Shogun. The Isuzu Trooper is arguably the most versatile Japanese off-roader on the UK market. In its first year, International Motors pitched the prices very competitively (that's sales jargon for low) to entice people away from other marques; prices have since risen, but the Trooper is still likely to win friends and influence off-roaders.

When it comes to prices, this author believes that Daihatsu would do a lot better if they lowered them! Daihatsu followed the Suzuki policy of 'testing the water' in the UK principally with commercial versions with small underpowered engines, liked what they found out, and then entered the fray with an extremely distinctive Fourtrak model range. As four-wheel drives tend to look very similar, something as distinctive as the Daihatsu Fourtrak Estate is always likely to find a following. The Daihatsu range has SWB and LWB models, but even the Estate version is not as large as either the Shogun or the Trooper, although it is bigger

Toyota Landcruiser: new version, restyled and with coil springs, has sold well in other countries and is now poised to make its mark here, too.

than the Suzuki — a sort of in-between size, really. Petrol, diesel and turbo diesel are the engine options, the diesels being particularly smooth and efficient units, although the petrol engines perhaps could do with a little more power. Running costs of the diesel versions are low, which to some extent compensates for the higher initial prices.

The Daihatsu Fourtrak does have its limitations, because while it incorporates some forward thinking visually, underneath it is primitive, with leaf springs all round, making it a very dated design. Daihatsu are not alone in using them, and it took Land Rover 22 years to design a vehicle that dispensed with them, but that's no excuse. When you have leaf springs on the front, wheel travel is restricted — you just cannot get a leaf spring to 'give' enough. It also limits the vehicle's turning circle, which is more of a problem on than off-road. To be fair, though, the Daihatsu's leaf springs are remarkably supple to the extent that a Panhard rod has to be used to locate the front axle. There's also an anti-roll bar to limit the wallowing and roll when cornering. All this, however, limits the off-road abilities, and Daihatsu aren't blind to these problems as they have fitted an over-complex microprocessor-controlled three-stage damper system. An electrical actuator is fitted to the top of each shock absorber, which allows you to adjust the damper's valving. A Hard, Soft or Normal setting is available at the touch of a switch, although you would be hard pushed to notice much difference. If the Fourtrak is driven hard around country lanes it handles better with the setting on Hard, but off-road it is impossible to notice any difference. Just a gimmick? Maybe not; the Japanese usually know what they are doing, and this could just be the initial testing of a far more sophisticated idea. May I suggest coil springs?

It's coil springs that make the latest Toyota Landcruiser such an important new model in the UK. The big old diesel Landcruiser is something of an old friend. Reliable and exceedingly roomy, it has a front that looks like a 1950s truck (the latest versions are slightly better) and it has those leaf springs. . . . In its favour there is a six-cylinder diesel engine that has torque of monumental ability right from tickover. While the suspension and long wheelbase coupled with only reasonable ground clearance do limit off-road ability, a good driver can use the torque of the engine to drag this beast through some very impressive and difficult terrain. But it is a dated design.

Landcruiser II, on the other hand, has coil springs, is SWB and has a turbo diesel engine. It also has a background of great sales success in other parts of the world, including Europe (it's a top seller in France, for instance) so it's not an unknown quantity, although at the time of writing we have yet to get complete knowledge of it in the UK. Why have Toyota been so shy in bringing it in? The answer is a simple case of economics;

Nissan Patrol: updated body, capable, well equipped, light and easy to use – but its successor could be the *really* important model.

they are restricted by the Japanese import quota and their cars have been doing so well that they have not considered it necessary. While predictions are always dangerous, it seems likely that sooner or later the new Landcruiser will find a strong following in the UK and sales and demand will be high. Quality will come through, especially as the UK market gets more educated about four-wheel drive. When you get stuck somewhere in a leaf-sprung machine only to watch someone else with coil springs sail through the same section, you do begin to wonder if it's time for a change, and the Japanese usually have the answer.

Nissan do, for instance. As this is being written, Nissan have just unveiled an entirely new Patrol with coil springs and a completely new body and interior. In fact the new Patrol is *all* new. The bad news is that it is not likely to come into the UK for a while, not that there's that much wrong with the old one. It is capable and it matches the others. In many respects it is like the original Landcruiser — especially the version with the 3.2-litre diesel engine. Both SWB and LWB models are available in the UK, with leaf springs all round, are well-equipped and, typical of all Japanese off-roaders, light and easy to use. Like the Suzuki, they come into the UK from the Santana factory in Spain, but this doesn't make them any cheaper. Until the new Patrol comes to the UK, Nissan is something of a sleeping giant in the British off-road scene.

Mercedes-Benz is another giant, of course. Better known for its high-

21

quality — and expensive — saloon cars, the German manufacturer's entry into the off-road market has not been quite as successful. The Gelandewagen has been with us in the UK since 1980, but sales figures have been lower than one would have expected. Mercedes, indeed, have suffered from their own reputation. If a company of their stature is to produce a four-wheel drive machine it is natural that it should compete against the very best, *i.e.* the Range Rover. Certainly it competes on prices, but questions remain over its appearance and off-road ability. On a personal note, the G-Wagen's appearance certainly grows on you; it is not ugly — solid, teutonic, even militaristic, perhaps, but not ugly. Although expensive, you get a build quality that unfortunately Range Rover is not always able to match, let alone beat.

Live axles plus coil springs give good suspension movement, but with the front anti roll bar it is not as good as a Range Rover in this respect. It also differs from the Range Rover in that it has lockable differentials for the front and rear axles. These are useful, but they should be engaged *before* you need them. Failing to engage them before you are completely stuck will usually mean that you simply dig yourself deeper into your problem. It is often sufficient to lock the rear and leave the front free — locking the front does restrict the steering somewhat.

Developed for Mercedes-Benz by Steyr-Puch in Austria, the G-Wagen is solid, functional, and, as you would expect, very well built.

Lada Niva, here in Cossack form: very tough, compact, and a good performer off-road, the Niva has a lot going for it.

The Dacia Duster from Romania, powered by a licence-built Renault engine – cheap and cheerful, quite strong, but uncertain build quality.

The G-Wagen has selectable four-wheel drive, SWB and LWB versions are available, as are diesel and petrol engines. Here, too, people have their reservations. The 3-litre diesel is rather sluggish, a fact that Mercedes themselves have recognized; they have introduced a new 2.5-litre diesel engine in Germany. The petrol engines — 2.3 and 2.8-litre — come from the car side of the company, and are relatively thirsty and need to be revved rather higher than you would like in off-road conditions. You cannot use that light touch that the Land Rover V8 engine will allow and this can be a disadvantage off-road. As we have said, however, they are superbly built. There is a new model on the way, probably for 1989, and it is likely that Mercedes have taken into account all the criticisms levelled at the present G-Wagen. The next model really could be something.

For something completely different we move to Russia and Romania. Lada cars have something of a reputation in the UK for solid dependability, which has made them popular with older people. Indeed, the Russian saloons seem to have sold particularly well to those who have retired. If such an image prevents you from looking at the Lada Niva as an off-road choice, you'd be missing out. For a basic, relatively cheap machine there's a certain amount of sophistication built into the Niva — it's a good performer off-road. Only available in SWB form, it follows the almost ideal design of having 'a wheel at each corner', therefore leaving little or no front or rear overhang. The suspension is by independent coil springs and wishbones at the front and coil springs on a live axle at the rear. Four-wheel drive is permanent, a differential unit splitting the power between front and rear. The Niva also has 9in of ground clearance and good wheel travel, and although it is a bit of a handful as the steering is heavy and the controls somewhat awkward to a Western driver, it has a lot going for it. You feel that breaking a Niva would be difficult and little seems to stop it in normal off-road conditions.

Looks are very important in the off-road market and the UK importers clearly felt that the little Niva needed a boost, hence the Cossack version. This saw a special paint job with fancy seat covers and a sports steering wheel, spot lights, etc, which obviously pleases some people, even though it might not be to everybody's taste.

No-one can deny that the Niva is a good off-road option, but this is more than can be said of the Dacia Duster from Romania. Eastern bloc manufacturers have a problem when trying to sell cars in the West because we expect good build quality, and this is not forthcoming from the Dacia Duster. Despite valiant attempts to iron out the problems by the British importers, we have to say that they have not been successful; it is not a well-built vehicle. Off-road, the mechanicals are quite strong,

Above: Jeep CJ-5 Renegade: flamboyant successor to the little Willys vehicle that really started it all. Below: Land Rover that might have been – the one-off Cariba 'concept car' of 1987.

and an independent front end helps the leaf springs at the rear, but the Duster comes on tiny 14in wheels, which do not help much. Some people are attracted by the appearance and the bright colours in which the Dusters are available, but this cannot disguise the fact that there are better vehicles on the market for similar money.

Officially, there are no American off-roaders on the UK market. That must tell you something. There is, however, an active Jeep following over here (turn to the *Joining a club* section for more details). New Jeeps have to be personally imported into the UK because the vehicles do not meet all our National Type Approval regulations. The newest model is the Jeep Wrangler and when imported here all the extras put it in the same price category as a top-of-the-range Shogun, nudging the cheapest Mercedes-Benz, so you need to be a real Jeep enthusiast to want a new one. Selectable four-wheel drive with a column-change automatic gearbox is typically American, but the Wrangler has a wonderfully torquey engine that will pull you out of many tight spots. It certainly has a style of its own with a lot of chrome and flashy bits.

But that's what makes four-wheel drive so special. There is such a wide variety of vehicles on offer, each with its own distinct character, covering a wide range of prices, specifications and levels of performance to suit so many different needs. There's bound to be one that appeals to you.

BFGOODRICH T/A® RADIALS

THE RESULTS SPEAK FOR THEMSELVES

Specially-developed for both on and off-road use, the BFGoodrich Radial All-Terrain T/A has proved unbeatable in the roughest environments.

Recently updated with an even more rugged construction and new self-cleaning tread, the second generation Radial All-Terrain T/A gives tremendous traction on loose slippery terrain, better puncture resistance and higher mileage than before, yet still provides a comfortable ride and a reassuring grip on the road.

And if the going is even tougher, there's the BFGoodrich Radial Mud-Terrain T/A. With a similar construction, and a wide, open tread pattern, it's designed to conquer the stickiest situation.

Both the Radial All-Terrain T/A and Radial Mud-Terrain T/A are available in a wide range of sizes for almost any 4 × 4, pick-up and light truck.

Please send me further information and details of my nearest stockist.
Name:
Address:
Tel:
Vehicle: Year:

---✂

SOUTH & SOUTH WEST

CHESSINGTON TYRES LTD
Bordon Trading Estate, Bordon
Hampshire, GU35 9HH
☎ (04203) 89918/9

MIDLANDS & THE NORTH

SOUTHAM TYRES LTD
Southam Drive, Southam
Warwickshire, CV33 0JH
☎ (092681) 3888

"Try and judge the depth"

On-road or off-road. Suzuki keep you on the right road.

Finding the right way round obstacles is great fun – especially in a Suzuki.

That's why we have produced a booklet of '4 x 4 driving tips' to go with our superb range of light weight 4-wheel drive vehicles.

It's free on request – just ring the Suzuki Information Centre on 01-636 0100. You will receive our latest range brochure too! Just to make sure that before venturing off road – you're on the right road – in a Suzuki.

2

Facts and figures

In the following pages we've gathered together brief specifications of a representative selection of both four-wheel drive off-road vehicles and 4x4 cars. We've tried to include all the major contenders on the UK market as well as one or two of the smaller volume imports, and for those vehicles with a long history there are some notes on the earlier versions as well as the range current at the time of writing. The available variety is large and widening quite rapidly, so it is inevitable that we have had to leave some possiblities out because space is not unlimited, but we think we've provided the basic information you need to compare and contrast the different ways of going four-wheel drive.

By their very nature, four-wheel drives tend to be offered in various versions and with a variety of optional equipment. Manufacturers and importers make their decisions about what combinations to offer, which engine in which wheelbase and so on, for marketing as well as engineering reasons, and consequently they can – and do – change their minds from one year to the next. So we can't list every permutation – the forty years of Land Rover history, for example, is a good subject for a book on its own. For similar reasons, though we've made every effort to be accurate, we cannot accept responsibility if any particular figure fails to match an individual vehicle.

The equipment fitted to a vehicle and its precise specification are important points to consider if you are assessing the value of a possible secondhand purchase. Another point to watch is spares availability: there have been some intriguing ex-military machines and unusual imports on the market from time to time, but you could be in trouble if you need replacement bits. The major importers are well established here, though, and the growing number of specialists offering accessories and add-on fittings ensures that there is something to suit every taste.

Audi Quattro

Engine: 5 cyl, 2,144cc, turbo, 200bhp at 5,500rpm, 210lb/ft at 3,500rpm.
Transmission: 5 speed manual, permanent 4WD.
Suspension: MacPherson struts all round.
Dimensions: wheelbase 2,525mm, 99.4in; length 4,420mm, 174in; width 1,723mm, 67.8in; height 1,346mm, 53in; kerb weight 1,300kg, 2,867lb.

Audi 80/90 quattro

Engine: 80; 4 cyl, 1,781cc, 112bhp at 5,800rpm, 118lb/ft at 3,400rpm. 90; 5 cyl, 2,226cc, 136bhp at 5,700rpm, 137lb/ft at 3,500rpm.
Transmission: 5 speed manual, permanent 4WD.
Suspension: MacPherson struts all round.
Dimensions: wheelbase 2,535mm, 99.8in; length 4,395mm, 173in; width 1,695mm, 66.7in; height 1,395mm, 55in; kerb weight 1,140kg, 2,510lb.

Audi 200 Avant quattro

Engine: 5 cyl, 2,144cc, turbo, 182bhp at 5,700rpm, 186lb/ft at 3,600rpm.
Transmission: 5 speed manual, permanent 4WD.
Suspension: MacPherson struts front, wishbones rear.
Dimensions: wheelbase 2,685mm, 105.7in; length 4,805mm, 189in; width 1,815mm, 71.5in; height 1,420mm, 56in; kerb weight 1,450kg, 3,196lb.

BMW 325iX

Engine: 6 cyl, 2,494cc, 171bhp at 5,800rpm, 167lb/ft at 4,300rpm.
Transmission: 5 speed manual, 4 speed auto option, permanent 4WD.
Suspension: MacPherson struts front, semi-trailing arms rear.
Dimensions: wheelbase 2,570mm, 101in; length 4,325mm, 170in; width 1,660mm, 65in; height 1,400mm, 55in; kerb weight 1,255kg, 2,766lb.

Dacia Duster

Engine: 4 cyl, 1,397cc, 65bhp at 5,300rpm, 77lb/ft at 3,300rpm.
Transmission: 4 speed manual, hi-lo transfer, selectable 4WD, manual freewheel hubs.
Suspension: wishbones front; live axle, leaf springs, rear.
Dimensions: wheelbase 2,400mm, 94.5in; length 3,785mm, 149in; width 1,600mm, 63in; height 1,727mm, 68in; kerb weight 1,200kg, 2,645lb.

Daihatsu Fourtrak range

Petrol engine: 4 cyl, 1,998cc, 87bhp at 4,600rpm, 116lb/ft at 3,000rpm.
Diesel engine: 4 cyl, 2,765cc, 72bhp at 3,800rpm, 125lb/ft at 2,200rpm.
Turbo diesel engine: 4 cyl, 2,765cc, turbo, 87bhp at 3,600rpm, 155lb/ft at 2,200rpm; 1988 model, 90bhp at 3,400rpm, 165lb/ft at 2,200rpm.
Transmission: 5 speed manual, hi-lo transfer, selectable 4WD, manual freewheel hubs.
Suspension: live axles, leaf springs.
Dimensions, SWB: wheelbase 2,205mm, 86.8in; length 3,800mm, 149.6in; width 1,580mm, 62.2in; height 1,915mm, 75.4in; kerb weight 1,230 to 1,480kg, 2,712 to 3,263lb.
Dimensions, LWB: wheelbase 2,530mm, 99.6in; length 4,065mm, 160in; width 1,580mm, 62.2in; height 1,915mm, 75.4in; kerb weight 1,230 to 1,480kg, 2,712 to 3,263lb.
Dimensions, pick-up: wheelbase 2,800mm, 110.2in; length 4,435mm, 174.6in; width 1,580mm, 62.2in; height 1,830mm, 72in; kerb weight 1,530kg, 3,374lb; payload 1,000kg, 2,205lb.

Fiat Panda 4x4 Fire

Engine: 4 cyl, 999cc, 50bhp at 5,500rpm, 58lb/ft at 3,000rpm.
Transmission: 5 speed manual, crawler first, selectable 4WD.
Suspension: MacPherson struts front; live axle, leaf springs, rear.
Dimensions: wheelbase 2,170mm, 85.4in; length 3,410mm, 134.2in; width 1,500mm, 59in; height 1,470mm, 58in; kerb weight 790kg, 1,742lb.

Ford Sierra XR4x4

Engine: V6, 2,792cc, 150bhp at 5,700rpm, 159lb/ft at 3,800rpm.
Transmission: 5 speed manual, permanent 4WD.
Suspension: MacPherson struts front, semi-trailing arms rear.
Dimensions: wheelbase 2,610mm, 102.8in; length 4,425mm, 174.2in; width 1,720mm, 67.7in; height 1,360mm, 53.5in; kerb weight 1,270kg, 2,800lb.

Ford Sierra XR4x4 Estate

Engine: V6, 2,792cc, 150bhp at 5,700rpm, 159lb/ft at 3,800rpm.
Transmission: 5 speed manual, permanent 4WD.
Suspension: MacPherson struts front, semi-trailing arms rear.
Dimensions: wheelbase 2,610mm, 102.8in; length 4,510mm, 177.5in; width 1,720mm, 67.7in; height 1,385mm, 54.5in; kerb weight 1,270kg, 2,800lb.

Ford Granada 2.9i Scorpio 4x4

Engine: V6, 2,933cc, 150bhp at 5,700rpm, 172lb/ft at 3,000rpm.
Transmission: 5 speed manual, permanent 4WD.
Suspension: MacPherson struts front, semi-trailing arms rear.
Dimensions: wheelbase 2,765mm, 108.8in; length 4,670mm, 184in; width 1,760mm, 69.3in; height 1,430mm, 56.5in; kerb weight 1,422kg, 3,135lb.

Honda Civic Shuttle Real Time 4WD

Engine: 4 cyl, 1,488cc, 85bhp at 6,000rpm, 93lb/ft at 3,500rpm.
Transmission: 6 speed manual, VC-engaged 4WD.
Suspension: MacPherson struts front; live axle, coil springs, rear.
Dimensions: wheelbase 2,450mm, 96.5in; length 4,080mm, 160.6in; width 1,645mm, 64.8in; height 1,510mm, 59.4in; kerb weight 970kg, 2,138lb.

Isuzu Trooper range

2.3 petrol engine: 4 cyl, 2,254cc, 88bhp at 4,600rpm, 123lb/ft at 2,500rpm.
2.6i petrol engine: 4 cyl, 2,559cc, 111bhp at 5,000rpm, 138lb/ft at 2,500rpm.
2.2 diesel engine: 4 cyl, 2,238cc, turbo, 72bhp at 4,600rpm, 114lb/ft at 2,500rpm.
2.8 diesel engine: 4 cyl, 2,771cc, turbo, 95bhp at 3,700rpm, 153lb/ft at 2,100rpm.
Transmission: 5 speed manual, hi-lo transfer, selectable 4WD, auto freewheel hubs.
Suspension: wishbones, torsion bars, front; live axle, leaf springs, rear.
Dimensions, SWB: wheelbase 2,300mm, 90.6in; length 4,120mm, 162.2in; width 1,650mm, 65in; height 1,800mm, 71in; kerb weight 1,480 to 1,660kg, 3,263 to 3,660lb.
Dimensions, LWB: wheelbase 2,650mm, 104.3in; length 4,470mm, 176in; width 1,650mm, 65in; height 1,800mm, 71in; kerb weight 1,620 to 1,720kg, 3,571 to 3,792lb.

Lada Niva

Engine: 4 cyl, 1,569cc, 78bhp at 5,400rpm, 88lb/ft at 3,200rpm.
Transmission: 5 speed manual, hi-lo transfer, permanent 4WD.
Suspension: wishbones front; live axle, coil springs, rear.
Dimensions: wheelbase 2,200mm, 86.6in; length 3,720mm, 146.5in; width 1,680mm, 66in; height 1,640mm, 64.5in; kerb weight 1,150kg, 2,535lb.

Lancia Delta HF 4WD

Engine: 4 cyl, 1,995cc, turbo, 165bhp at 5,250rpm, 210lb/ft at 2,750rpm.
Transmission: 5 speed manual, permanent 4WD, centre VC, rear Torsen diff.
Suspension: MacPherson struts all round.
Dimensions: wheelbase 2,475mm, 97.4in; length 3,895mm, 153.4in; width 1,620mm, 63.8in; height 1,380mm, 54.3in; kerb weight 1,190kg, 2,623lb.

Lancia Delta HF integrale

Engine: 4 cyl, 1,995cc, 185bhp at 5,300rpm, 224lb/ft at 2,500rpm.
Transmission: 5 speed manual, permanent 4WD, centre VC, Torsen diff.
Suspension: MacPherson struts all round.
Dimensions: wheelbase 2,480mm, 97.6in; length 3,900mm, 153.5in; width 1,700mm, 66.9in; height 1,380mm, 54.3in; kerb weight 1,200kg, 2,645lb.

Land Rover range

Petrol engines, 4 cyl: 1948-1951; 1,595cc, 50bhp at 4,000rpm, 80lb/ft at 2,000rpm. 1952-1958; 1,997cc, 52bhp at 4,000rpm, 101lb/ft at 1,500rpm. 1958-1985; 2,286cc, 70bhp at 4,000rpm, 120lb/ft at 1,500rpm. 1983-1985 (One Ten and Ninety); 2,286cc, 74bhp at 4,000rpm, 120lb/ft at 2,000rpm. From 1985; 2,494cc, 83bhp at 4,000rpm, 133lb/ft at 2,000rpm.

Petrol engine, 6 cyl: 1967-1980; 2,625cc, 83bhp at 4,500rpm, 128lb/ft at 1,500rpm.

Petrol engines, V8: 1979-1985 (Series III); 3,528cc, 91bhp at 3,500rpm, 166lb/ft at 2,000rpm. 1983-1986 (One Ten and Ninety); 3,528cc, 114bhp at 4,000rpm, 185lb/ft at 2,500rpm. From 1986; 3,528cc, 134bhp at 5,000rpm, 187lb/ft at 2,500rpm.

Diesel engines, 4 cyl: 1957-1961; 2,052cc, 51bhp at 3,500rpm, 87lb/ft at 2,000rpm. 1962-1984; 2,286cc, 62bhp at 4,000rpm, 103lb/ft at 1,800rpm. 1984-1986; 2,494cc, 67bhp at 4,000rpm, 114lb/ft at 1,800rpm. From 1986; 2,494cc, turbo, 85bhp at 4,000rpm, 150lb/ft at 1,800rpm.

Transmission: 5 speed manual (4 speed, earlier models), hi-lo transfer, permanent or selectable 4WD according to model.

Suspension: live axles; leaf springs, earlier models; coil springs, One Ten and Ninety.

Dimensions, earlier models: Wheelbase 80in, 2,032mm; length 132in, 3,353mm. Wheelbase 86in, 2,184mm; length 140.7in, 3,574mm. Wheelbase 88in, 2,235mm; length 140.8in, 3,576mm. Wheelbase 107in, 2,718mm; length 173.5in, 4,407mm. Wheelbase 109in, 2,769mm; length 175in, 4,445mm.

Dimensions, One Ten: wheelbase 2,794mm, 110in; length 4,445mm, 175in, to 4,674mm, 184in; width 1,791mm, 70.5in; height 2,035mm, 80.1in; kerb weight 1,734 to 1,774kg, 3,824 to 3,912lb.

Dimensions, Ninety: wheelbase 2,360mm, 92.9in; length 3,721mm, 146.5in; width 1,791mm, 70.5in; height 1,971mm, 77.6in; kerb weight 1,697 to 1,737kg, 3,741 to 3,829lb.

Range Rover

Petrol engine: V8, 3,532cc, Vogue (fuel injection), 165bhp at 4,750rpm, 207lb/ft at 3,000rpm; with carburettors, 127bhp at 4,000rpm, 194lb/ft at 2,500rpm; earlier models, 125 to 135bhp according to equipment.

Diesel engine: 4 cyl, 2,393cc, turbo, 112bhp at 4,200rpm, 183lb/ft at 2,000rpm.

Transmission: 5 speed manual, 4 speed ZF auto option; earlier models, 4 speed manual, 3 speed Chrysler auto option; hi-lo transfer, permanent 4WD.

Suspension: live axles, coil springs.

Dimensions: wheelbase 2,540mm, 100in; length 4,450mm, 175in; width 1,829mm, 72in; height 1,803mm, 71in; kerb weight 1,920 to 2,012kg, 4,233 to 4,435lb.

Mazda 323 Turbo 4x4

Engine: 4 cyl, 1,597cc, turbo, 148bhp at 6,000rpm, 144lb/ft at 5,000rpm.
Transmission: 5 speed manual, permanent 4WD, centre diff lock.
Suspension: MacPherson struts all round.
Dimensions: wheelbase 2,400mm, 94.5in; length 3,990mm, 157in; width 1,645mm, 64.8in; height 1,390mm, 54.7in; kerb weight 1,060 to 1,175kg, 2,337 to 2,590lb.

Mercedes-Benz G-Wagen

280GE petrol engine: 6 cyl, 2,746cc, 150bhp at 5,250rpm, 166lb/ft at 4,250rpm.
230GE petrol engine: 4 cyl, 2,299cc, 125bhp at 5,000rpm, 142lb/ft at 4,000rpm.
300GD diesel engine: 5 cyl, 2,998cc, 88bhp at 4,400rpm, 126lb/ft at 2,400rpm.
Transmission: 4 or 5 speed manual or 4 speed auto, hi-lo transfer, selectable 4WD, diff locks front and rear.
Suspension: live axles, coil springs.
Dimensions, SWB: wheelbase 2,400mm, 94.5in; length 3,955mm, 155.7in; width 1,700mm, 66.9in; height 1,970mm, 77.6in; kerb weight 1,935kg, 4,266lb.
Dimensions, LWB: wheelbase 2,850mm, 112.2in; length 4,405mm, 173.4in; width 1,700mm, 66.9in; height 1,970mm, 77.6in; kerb weight 2,055kg, 4,530lb.

Mitsubishi Shogun range

Petrol engine: 4 cyl, 2,555cc, 103bhp at 4,500rpm, 142lb/ft at 2,500rpm.
Diesel engine: 4 cyl, 2,477cc, turbo, 84bhp at 4,200rpm, 148lb/ft at 2,000rpm.
Transmission: 5 speed manual (4 speed auto option with diesel), hi-lo transfer, selectable 4WD, auto freewheel hubs.
Suspension: wishbones, torsion bars, front; live axle, leaf springs, rear.
Dimensions, SWB: wheelbase 2,350mm, 92.5in; length 3,995mm, 157.3in; width 1,680mm, 66.1in; height 1,840mm, 72.4in; kerb weight 1,450 to 1,640kg, 3,196 to 3,615lb.
Dimensions, LWB: wheelbase 2,695mm, 106.1in; length 4,600mm, 181.1in; width 1,680mm, 66.1in; height 1,945mm, 76.6in; kerb weight 1,740 to 1,840kg, 3,836 to 4,056lb.

Nissan Patrol range

Petrol engine: 6 cyl, 2,753cc, 120bhp at 4,800rpm, 149lb/ft at 3,200rpm.
Diesel engine: 6 cyl, 3,246cc, 95bhp at 3,600rpm, 160lb/ft at 1,800rpm.
Transmission: 4 speed or 5 speed manual, hi-lo transfer, selectable 4WD, auto freewheel hubs.
Suspension: live axles, leaf springs.
Dimensions, SWB: wheelbase 2,350mm, 92.5in; length 4,070mm, 160.2in; width 1,690mm, 66.5in; height 1,845mm, 72.6in; kerb weight 1,860 to 1,930kg, 4,100 to 4,255lb.
Dimensions, LWB: wheelbase 2,970mm, 117in; length 4,690mm, 184.6in; width 1,690mm, 66.5in; height 1,805mm, 71.1in; kerb weight 1,860 to 1,930kg, 4,100 to 4,255lb.

Subaru 1.8 range

Engine: flat 4 cyl, 1,781cc, 80bhp at 6,000rpm, 101lb/ft at 3,000rpm; turbo, 134bhp at 5,600rpm, 147lb/ft at 2,800rpm.

Transmission: 5 speed manual (auto option some models), hi-lo transfer, permanent or selectable 4WD according to model.

Suspension: MacPherson struts front; semi-trailing arms rear.

Dimensions: wheelbase 2,470mm, 97.2in. Length, estate, 4,410mm, 174in; coupe 4,495mm, 177in. Width, estate 1,661mm, 65.4in; coupe 1,701mm, 67in. Height, estate 1,490mm, 58.7in; coupe 1,346mm, 53in. Kerb weight 1,134 to 1,224kg, 2,500 to 2,700lb.

Subaru Justy

Engine: 3 cyl, 1,190cc, 68bhp at 5,600rpm, 71lb/ft at 3,600rpm.

Transmission: 5 speed manual, selectable 4WD.

Suspension: MacPherson struts all round.

Dimensions: wheelbase 2,285mm, 90in; length 3,535mm, 139in; width 1,535mm, 60.4in; height 1,390mm, 55in; kerb weight 757kg, 1,669lb.

Suzuki LJ80

Engine: 4 cyl, 797cc, 39bhp at 5,750rpm, 44lb/ft at 3,500rpm.

Transmission: 4 speed manual, hi-lo transfer, selectable 4WD.

Suspension: live axles, leaf springs.

Dimensions: wheelbase 1,930mm, 76in; length 3,195mm, 126in; width 1,395mm, 54.5in; height 1,690mm, 66.5in; kerb weight 800 to 820kg, 1,764 to 1,808lb.

Suzuki SJ410, Santana

Engine: 4 cyl, 970cc, 45bhp at 5,500rpm, 54lb/ft at 3,000rpm.
Transmission: SJ, 4 speed manual; Santana, 5 speed manual; hi-lo transfer, selectable 4WD, manual freewheel hubs.
Suspension: live axles, leaf springs.
Dimensions: wheelbase 2,030mm, 79.9in; length 3,440mm, 135.4in; width 1,460mm, 57.5in; height 1,680mm, 66.1in; kerb weight 890kg, 1,960lb.

Suzuki SJ413K pick-up

Engine: 4 cyl, 1,324cc, 64bhp at 6,000rpm, 74lb/ft at 3,500rpm.
Transmission: 5 speed manual, hi-lo transfer, selectable 4WD.
Suspension: live axles, leaf springs.
Dimensions: wheelbase 2,375mm, 93.5in; length 4,010mm, 157.9in; width 1,460mm, 57.5in; height 1,680mm, 66.1in; kerb weight 915kg, 2,017lb.

Toyota Landcruiser

Diesel engine: 6 cyl, 3,980cc, 99bhp at 3,500rpm, 171lb/ft at 1,800rpm.
Transmission: 5 speed manual or 4 speed auto, hi-lo transfer, selectable 4WD, manual freewheel hubs.
Suspension: live axles, leaf springs.
Dimensions: wheelbase 2,730mm, 107.5in; length 4,750mm, 187in; width 1,800mm, 70.9in; height 1,800mm, 70.9in; kerb weight 2,070kg, 4,565lb.

Toyota Landcruiser II

Diesel engine: 4 cyl, 2,446cc, turbo, 84 bhp at 4,000rpm, 138lb/ft at 2,400rpm.
Transmission: 5 speed manual, hi-lo transfer, selectable 4WD, manual freewheel hubs, limited-slip diffs.
Suspension: live axles, coil springs.
Dimensions: wheelbase 2,310mm, 91in; length 4,060mm, 160in; width 1,790mm, 70.5in; height 1,885mm, 74.2in; kerb weight 1,810kg, 3,990lb.

Toyota Tercel 4WD Estate

Engine: 4 cyl, 1,453cc, 71bhp at 5,600rpm, 83lb/ft at 2,400rpm.
Transmission: 5 speed manual, crawler low, selectable 4WD.
Suspension: MacPherson struts front; live axle, coil springs, rear.
Dimensions: wheelbase 2,430mm, 95.6in; length 4,175mm, 164in; width 1,615mm, 63.6in; height 1,510mm, 59.4in; kerb weight 1,000kg, 2,206lb.

Toyota Corolla 4WD Estate

Engine: 4 cyl, 1,587cc, 94bhp at 6,000rpm, 100lb/ft at 3,600rpm.
Transmission: 5 speed manual, permanent 4WD, centre diff lock.
Suspension: MacPherson struts front; live axle, coil springs, rear.
Dimensions: wheelbase 2,430mm, 95.6in; length 4,250mm, 167.3in; width 1,665mm, 65.5in; height 1,485mm, 58.5in; kerb weight 1,185kg, 2,612lb.

3

Mind your language

If you listen to a group of off-roaders talking together, you could be forgiven for not understanding what they are going on about. There's a lot of jargon concerned with the subject and to the outsider it may all sound rather complicated. It's not. And, more to the point, there are a number of well-meaning enthusiasts who, while they use all the right names, don't always know what they mean. This section, therefore, is intended to remedy all that and help you through the maze.

TRANSFER BOX
One thing that makes your four-wheel drive different from all the ordinary cars on the road is that you have what amounts to a second gearbox. The transfer box is the additional gearbox that enables drive to be transferred to all four wheels. The transfer box accepts drive from the main gearbox and divides it to the two axles, front and rear. The actual position of the transfer box will vary from one four-wheel drive to another; it can be included in the main gearbox and is thus called integral, or set further back and be remotely mounted. In all popular off-roaders, the transfer box has two ratios, High and Low, which, as they work in series with the main gearbox, have the effect of doubling the number of ratios available. A five-speed box, therefore, has five High ratios (predominantly for use on the road) and five Low speeds (for off-road use). The transfer box can be 'part-time', which allows you to select two-wheel drive only for road use. This is the case with the majority of Japanese off-roaders, the transfer box having three positions, 2H, 4H and 4L. Other transfer boxes work permanently, as in the Range Rover, and therefore only have two positions, 4H or 4L. In the latter case it also incorporates a lockable centre differential. Read on.

All vehicles with selectable four-wheel drive have two gear levers – the large one controls your normal four (or five) gears plus reverse, while the smaller stubby lever shifts from two-wheel drive into either High or Low ratio four-wheel drive.

LOCKABLE CENTRE DIFFERENTIAL

To transmit the drive to front and rear, the transfer box has a centre differential. In really adverse off-road conditions, the action of the centre differential added to the diffs in the front and rear axles can mean that forward progress can be halted if just one wheel starts to spin as nearly all the drive will be transmitted to that wheel. To counter this, it is possible to lock the centre differential, which effectively disables it. This is generally done by means of a splined, sliding coupling, which joins the front and rear outputs of the differential as one. Now, provided that at least one wheel on each axle has some traction, forward motion will continue. The Range Rover and the latest Land Rovers are the prime examples of vehicles with lockable centre differentials. A bright orange warning light is fitted to many models as it is important that you do not drive on dry tarmac with the centre diff locked, otherwise you could suffer transmission wind-up.

DIFF LOCKS

It follows quite logically that if it is possible to lock up the centre differential, why not the diffs in the front and rear axles? Mercedes-Benz are the champions of this particular off-road strategy, and it's something that can lead to many hours of endless discussion. Why do Mercedes-Benz favour axle diff locks and Land Rover ardently argue that they are more of a hindrance than a help? In simple terms, front and rear diff locks must be used correctly for them to be worthwhile. You must anticipate their need and select them before you get stuck. In the case of the Mercedes-Benz G-Wagen this is simply done by pulling up the suitable lever which hydraulically locks the diff. The arguments against their use are that if you get stuck and then try to lock the diff you just succeed in digging yourself into the mud. Also, locking the front diff does make the steering more difficult and less responsive. As with all off-road situations, it's a case of planning ahead to avoid the trouble; if you can do that, using diff locks can be a great help, but they can get the inexperienced driver into trouble on occasions.

TRANSMISSION WIND-UP

Let's go back to the basics for a moment. When a wheeled vehicle goes round a corner, the inside wheels travel a shorter distance than those on the outside. Now, if they are not being driven (front wheels on a rear-wheel drive car for instance) this doesn't matter, but connect them up to drive shafts and an engine and it is obviously important to allow one side to travel a different distance from the other; this, of course, is achieved by the use of a differential. Four-wheel drive vehicles have two differentials which can be connected. On full-time four-wheel drives the discrepancy in the turning circles is accounted for by the aid of the centre diff. The problem occurs when the centre diff is locked and you drive the vehicle on dry tarmac where there is no possibility of allowing the wheels to travel differing distances through bends. (The same problem will occur with a part-time four-wheel drive vehicle if 4WD is engaged.) The poor transmission components have to absorb the differences and they actually begin to twist or 'wind up'. At the very least this will lead to excessive tyre wear; at worst you will break something! Wind-up can occur off-road, but because there is always likely to be some wheel slip this build-up of forces can be dispersed. So remember, if you have a part-time system do not drive in four-wheel drive on dry tarmac, and if you have a permanent system make sure that the centre diff lock is disengaged on the road.

TRANSMISSION BRAKE

Land Rovers, Range Rovers and Suzukis are fitted with transmission brakes. This is an independent drum brake which is fitted to the rear output shaft of the transfer box and therefore provides a very efficient parking brake that will work on all four wheels (assuming, in the case of a part-time four-wheel drive system, that 4WD is engaged). This is obviously a much better system than the standard cable-operated brakes as it will hold a vehicle on severe slopes and in adverse conditions it avoids the need for potentially vulnerable cables running under the car. You should not, however, pull on this brake while the car is running — handbrake turns are out!

POWER TAKE OFF

Four-wheel drives are often working vehicles, being more than just a means of transport. To fulfil some of those working demands the engine is needed to be a source of power to operate auxiliary equipment, so many four-wheel drives can be fitted with power take off points (often just called PTOs) hydraulically driven from a transfer box-mounted pump. Land Rovers are the best examples of this, having PTO points on the transfer box and the engine.

If your four-wheel drive is fitted with a power take off working in the wilds presents few problems. This picture shows a hydraulic power take off fitted to a Land Rover in use to operate a chain saw.

GROUND CLEARANCE

There is far more to the term ground clearance than just being the distance between the vehicle's underpinnings and the ground. It is the distance that must always be considered in conjunction with the vehicle's wheelbase (the distance between the centres of the front and rear wheels) when you are assessing how effective a vehicle is likely to be off-road. The minimum ground clearance point on a four-wheel drive is usually from the bottom of the transfer case or the front or rear differential. On road cars the lowest point is often the exhaust, but a well-designed off-roader should have that particular item well out of harm's way.

When considering the rear of a four-wheel drive, the diff/axle set-up is a one-piece affair and therefore rises up and down with the rear wheels, so the ground clearance of this diff does not vary that much. Many modern four-wheel drives now have independent front suspension systems, which means that the vulnerable front diff is fixed to the chassis and the wheels move independently. As a result, the ground clearance beneath the front diff will vary considerably, and that's a great bonus.

Ground clearance can be increased by fitting larger tyres, but this may not be possible on your vehicle as larger tyres may not fit under the arches, or they may foul the bodywork when on full lock.

For anyone considering serious off-roading on rough rocky ground, where projections are likely to catch on differentials or transfer boxes, it is worth considering fitting skid plates for protection. These obviously don't increase the ground clearance (in many cases they lower it), but at least when you hear that heart-stopping metallic scraping noise of rock against metal you will be slightly comforted by the knowledge that it's your skid plate that's being dented, not your gearbox.

FREE WHEELING HUBS

Part-time four-wheel drives, especially Japanese ones, are fitted with free wheeling hubs. These disengage the front wheels either manually (as on the Daihatsu Fourtrak and early Suzuki SJ) or automatically (as on the Isuzu Trooper and Mitsubishi Shogun). The disconnection is at the hubs so the wheels do not turn the drive shafts when the vehicle is in two-wheel drive. It is claimed that this leads to savings of fuel and less wear of components. The automatic hubs lock as soon as you have selected four-wheel drive and are unlocked when you disengage and then reverse the vehicle for a yard or so. Manual hubs are rather basic as you have to get out of your car and twist them into the lock position. It must be remembered that in a Fourtrak or an older model Suzuki SJ, for instance, just slotting the transfer lever into 4H does *not* give you four-wheel drive until you switch those hubs; you'll be twisting the front prop

Manual freewheeling hubs must be switched to 'lock' before you attempt any off-road driving, otherwise, while you will be driving both axles, you won't be driving the front wheels. This picture shows a 1987 Daihatsu Fourtrack with manual freewheeling hubs.

Vehicles that have the word 'auto' on their front hubs, like this 1988 Mitsubishi Shogun, have automatic freewheel hubs that engage when the transfer lever is moved from two-wheel to four-wheel drive.

shaft and the drive shafts but not the wheels. Some people fit free wheeling hubs to the older (part-time four-wheel drive) Land Rovers.

GROUND ANCHORS
It is always best to go off-roading with at least one other vehicle, but

Ground anchors are essential if you are to do any serious off-roading, particularly when travelling in a group of two or more vehicles. You drive on to them and they dig in the mud; the vehicle is then almost immobile and can be used as an anchor to winch another out. To retrieve them, just reverse and they pull themselves out.

sometimes that is just not possible. If you get stuck, therefore, you have to get yourself free. Under such circumstances, ground anchors can be a great help. A ground anchor is a device that is driven into the ground to provide a secure anchorage point for a winch when no other is available. Proprietary ground anchors are available, but there are also ways of using your spare wheel, for instance, as a ground anchor (see *Tricks of the Trade*).

APPROACH AND DEPARTURE ANGLES

These angles are crucial to a vehicle's off-road ability. They relate to the maximum angle of inclination of a slope that a vehicle can approach (or leave) at a right angle without grounding the underside. It is obvious, therefore, that the angles are a function of the amount of front and rear overhang that a vehicle has fore (and aft) of the wheels. The ideal layout of a vehicle is often said to be one that has 'a wheel at each corner'. Departure angles are affected when a tow bar is fitted as it lowers the ground clearance at that point. Manufacturers often make great play of approach and departure angles with clever drawings in their brochures. It must be appreciated that these angles are really theoretical. Seldom is it possible for a vehicle to approach a slope on completely level ground and at a right angle.

RAMP BREAKOVER ANGLE

This is yet another figure for those people compiling glossy brochures. It's the angle of a ridge that a vehicle can cross (again at a right angle) without grounding any part of its underside. The angle, of course, is dependent on the vehicle's wheelbase; the longer the wheelbase the easier it is to ground the underside on ridges.

MAXIMUM GRADEABILITY

Maximum gradeability is a fancy way of saying the steepest slope that a vehicle will safely pull away on. Again, this is done for the specification charts as it assumes perfect conditions on the surface of the slope and perfect traction being available. The figure is calculated using gross vehicle weight.

INCLINOMETERS

Some would say that inclinometers are just a gimmick to frighten passengers. They are great fun, however, are regularly fitted to Japanese off-roaders, and are also available from accessory shops to fit yourself. Fastened to the facia, they work on the principle of the carpenter's spirit level showing how far you are tilting fore and aft and side to side. They do *not* tell you how far a vehicle will tilt before it falls over. Even

This vehicle is just about to experience the ramp breakover angle of this slope. As the driver crests the hill and the front wheels start to descend he stands a chance of catching the underside of the chassis on the ridge. He may even get stuck there.

The inclinometer shown here is just a gimmick, but still good fun. What you must not do, however, is use it to decide that the incline you are crossing is safe. Instead, read the ground, and leave the inclinometer to your passengers...

inclinometers that are fitted as standard equipment have no way of telling the condition of the ground, or what equipment you are carrying that might affect the vehicle's centre of gravity. Under laboratory conditions most vehicles will roll over at between 40 and 45deg. If you play with your inclinometer, never exceed 30deg. If you get yourself into a situation where you survive, say, a 35deg slope on a hard surface, don't assume that you can do it again. Different surfaces have different effects on a vehicle and if you are not too careful, you'll find your inclinometer flashing 'TILT — YOU ARE UPSIDE DOWN!'.

ATVs
There is a growing interest these days in what are called ATVs — all terrain vehicles. The initials ATV are sometimes used in the title of a vehicle, but principally they describe many off-road vehicles, regardless of the number of driven wheels; they may have more than four, on the other hand sometimes they are only two-wheel drive. The two and three-wheeled off-road bikes are ATVs, as are the highly efficient six and eight-wheel drive Argocats.

PORTAL AXLES
It is unlikely that a recreational off-roader would ever consider portal

axles. These are fitted to specialist off-road vehicles and involve the use of reduction gearboxes at each wheel. They can be employed to lift the axle way above the wheels themselves and provide a much greater ground clearance, and we're talking feet here, not inches. It's rather like having a car on stilts. The applications are primarily agricultural.

ENGINE BRAKING

No, this is not what happens when you over-rev your engine. Descending steep, slippery slopes is when you need engine braking. As we explain in the section on off-road driving techniques, you do not use the foot brake on these occasions, you use the torque characteristics of the engine to control your rate of descent. A slow-revving diesel engine has excellent engine braking capabilities. In Low first gear with the engine ticking over it will drop you down a slope with the minimum of fuss.

SUSPENSION TRAVEL

Off-roaders talk a great deal about suspension travel, and so they should because it can sort out a good vehicle from an ordinary one. In order to progress across rough terrain you need to keep your wheels on the ground. That's not as fatuous a remark as at first it sounds. Suspension travel is the individual up-and-down movement of each wheel. The

This dramatic picture of a Lada Niva descending a particularly steep slope shows the extreme suspension travel of the rear wheel.

53

Just look at the extreme angles of the wheels in these two pictures. They show exactly what is meant by suspension travel, and why having enough of it is essential for a successful off-roader.

Range Rover has exceptionally good suspension travel and this is one of the prime factors that makes it such a good off-road performer. But vehicles with solid axles have a problem; when one wheel drops the momentum of the axle lifts the opposing wheel — perhaps completely off the ground, where it's useless. Freedom from that effect is one advantage of all-round independent suspension, which means that each wheel can move up or down without affecting the movement of any other wheels.

4

Tricks of the trade

Four-wheel driving is unlike any other form of motoring. While it is possible to own a four-wheel drive, keep it parked outside your house, wash it on Sundays and have it regularly serviced in much the same way as your neighbour does with his Ford Escort, that's unlikely. At least, we hope it is. If you're reading this book, then you're not that sort of driver; you're a *user* driver.

Four-wheel drive vehicles are mechanically more interesting than next door's Ford Escort and, more importantly, you will enjoy driving yours in a variety of different environments. You are able to take your vehicle to places the Escort driver can only read about — provided you are well prepared.

Unfortunately, in the UK we do not have the wide expanses of off-road territory like Australia and America, so it's not really a case of having to survive days travelling across the desert or long weekends lost in the outback. However, it's still possible to get away from civilization — away from the tarmac road — so it is necessary to make sure the vehicle is well prepared. To help you we have divided this section into two parts; the preparation needed to avoid trouble, and what to do should you find yourself in it! While obviously it has not been possible to cover every eventuality, we have included a great many situations that concern the enthusiastic off-roader. Some of the real tricks, however, we'll leave to the experts like one Belgian competitor in the Paris-Dakar Rally. After taking a ridge far too fast, his Range Rover landed awkwardly and broke the mountings of the rear suspension. The occupants refused to be beaten by this and used their seat belts to *tie* the axle into position! They actually made it to the end of the rally. Now we don't recommend such action, but it serves to illustrate that off-roaders are resourceful people and determined to make it home.

AVOIDING TROUBLE

The Boy Scouts have got the right idea because, with due acknowledgement to Baden Powell, the off-roader's motto should also read 'Be Prepared'. It's no good getting into difficulty down some green lane, miles from the nearest garage, and muttering, 'If only I'd got a . . .'. You have got to take it with you, and while there are limits to what can be carried, there are some golden rules.

You can always tell an enthusiastic off-roader because at holiday time there's no room for the family's luggage — all the available space having been taken up with the 'just in case' items. We're not suggesting that you follow that example, so we've selected the top 10 items that all off-roaders should consider carrying.

1: *Jack.* All vehicles should come equipped with a jack, but it may not be suitable for serious off-road use. After all, it has been designed purely to enable you to change a wheel *on the road*. Have a good look at the standard jack supplied with your vehicle. If it's the bottle-type jack it could be useful off-road in emergencies, but if it's the scissors type (commonly fitted to road cars) it is close to hopeless. Think seriously

Rest assured, you will get stuck. The driver of this Shogun has bottomed out in the deep ruts of this lane. Thankfully, he has come prepared with a shovel. This acts as a firm base in the mud for the vehicle's standard bottle jack. The rear diff of the Shogun is caught; once clear of the mud he may be able to drive off the jack using the front wheels, or more dramatically raise the rear wheels out of the rut and on to the firm ground (this is a technique that can be employed using a Hi Lift jack but is unlikely to be possible with a standard bottle-type jack).

about a hydraulic jack or a Hi Lift jack. The latter is a heavy, mechanical jack, it is unwieldy and a little awkward to use until you get the hang of it, but it really works and can help you out of a number of difficult situations. For the serious off-roader, if it's suitable for your vehicle, it's a must. The main drawback is that it is a bumper jack, so you need a solid bumper to locate it (Land Rover, Range Rover and Jeep owners are OK). It's also big — 4ft long — and it weighs around 30lb, so it's difficult to stow away without it rattling around and damaging the upholstery.

As with most jacks, the foot of the Hi Lift is too small to use on soft ground, so always carry a piece of strong plywood or planking to use as a firm base. For sure when you get that off-road puncture, it'll be where it's impossible to locate the base of the jack on firm ground, so the planking will be essential. Oh, and it will be raining! If you get caught without a suitable piece of wood you can always use the head of your shovel because that is the second 'must' on our list.

2: *Shovel.* All off-roaders need to have a shovel, there's no argument about this. You *will* get stuck at some point and need to dig yourself out. If it's not mud, then it could be snow. Don't just wander into the garden shed and steal the trusty garden spade, that's not the answer. General opinion favours the diamond point variety of spade for off-roading as these are the strongest and work well in rocky ground where your garden spade would be useless. Don't be tempted to use a tiny shovel like the ones the Marines have on their back packs in all the best war movies. Even if it's a pain to stow away, when you come to using your shovel you'll be pleased if it's a decent size. It's a good idea to have one side of the blade sharpened slightly as this allows you to cut through vegetation and undergrowth. Make sure it is stowed away securely (rubber bungy straps are the best idea) otherwise if it rolls loose it can do nasty damage to upholstery and interior body panels.

3: *Tow rope.* A good jack, shovel and a tow rope are the three most important items in an off-roader's boot. Get yourself a decent length of rope, either man-made or natural fibre, and look after it. One day maybe it will be attached to another vehicle in order to pull you out of a problem, but perhaps more importantly it provides you with the potential to aid other motorists. A four-wheel drive can be the ideal recovery vehicle and if you've got a decent tow rope you can help a stranded motorist. It's not unheard of for four-wheel drivers to earn themselves a bob or two during the snowy winter months. . .

Check your rope regularly, especially after use. Check for external damage from chaffing on rough ground. If it gets wet, make sure that it dries out naturally. Dampness will encourage the growth of mould, which is obviously not a condition you want on a natural fibre rope, and

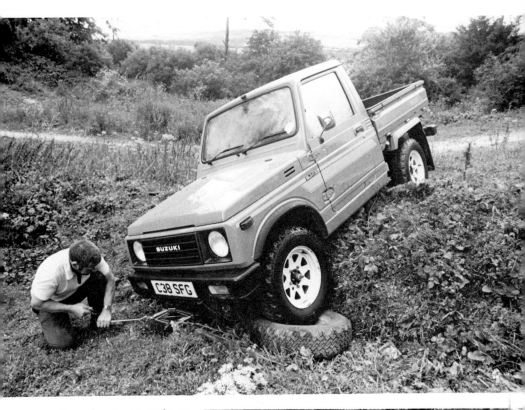

Ramp breakover angle, or look before you leap: this Suzuki pick-up has been caught on a very easy looking ridge and has become well and truly stuck. The answer is to raise the front in order to get the back down and restore some grip. With no other vehicles to assist (that's one golden rule broken) the spare wheel and the vehicle's scissor-type jack are used. From the rear, right, you can see that the Suzuki has bottomed out on the chassis. The driver is trying to put logs under the fully extended rear suspension to get the rear wheels to grip.

while it may not harm man-made ropes, moisture and mould can make them slippery to handle and could mean you pick up grit, which can cause abrasion. Keep your rope away from strong light, especially if it is the man-made fibre type.

4: *Torch.* When you have a problem, it will either be raining or it will be dark. Or it will be both. A lamp that is self-standing is better than a hand-held torch because you can place it somewhere in order to illuminate an area. Always carry a spare set of batteries.

5: *First aid kit.* All motorized vehicles should carry a first aid kit and in a vehicle that's going off-road and into the country it's far more likely that the occupants will get cut, scratched, stung or bitten. Obviously a proprietary kit will do the job, but add a few extras; pen, paper, adhesive tape, mirror and a bar of soap (the latter is useful not just for cleaning up but also for stopping fuel leaks, as will be explained later!). It's not a bad idea to attend a local first aid course. You are driving a vehicle that can help in simple recovery operations — cars in ditches and the like — so it would be useful to know how to treat the injured. Don't make the kit difficult to find, either. If it is out of sight, have a sign showing where it can be found — after all, you could just be an unconscious customer.

6: *Tool kit.* It can never be emphasized enough that when you take your vehicle off-road you will be working it hard. True, that's what it's been designed for, but if there's a weak link, it'll break off-road. Quite often these will be silly little things that can be mended on the spot — and quite often they'll need to be mended just to get you home. Make sure you have a good tool kit on board. Without spending vast sums of money on a complete new kit, be sensible and make sure that you've got a good *selection* of tools in the box; open-headed spanners rather than just ring or socket, a good pair of pliers, a mole wrench, screwdrivers, a hack-saw and a hammer (off-roaders use hammers a lot!).

7: *Kitchen sink.* Find yourself a tin or plastic container with a replaceable lid and fill it with screws, nuts and bolts, jubilee clips, washers, even nails. In fact, fill it with anything that's remotely automotive, and even things that aren't, like a couple of clothes pegs, hair grips (bachelors may have to buy these, the rest of you can 'acquire' them). It may seem a silly thing to do, but you'll be grateful later, we can guarantee it. All these little odds and ends will come in useful one day, that's for sure!

8: *Spray can.* A can of WD-40, or the equivalent, is always useful, not only to loosen those corroded nuts and bolts and fasteners, but also for spraying ignition wires to repel excessive moisture. There's always a lot of water about when you go off-road, and sometimes it gets just where you don't want it.

9: *Coat hanger.* A roll of wire is useful and will tie very difficult objects together for a strong temporary repair. If you haven't a roll of the 'proper stuff' throw in an old wire coat hanger, you'll find it has a great many uses.

10: *The Off Road and 4 Wheel Drive Handbook!* We couldn't forget this one could we? The aim with this book is for it to be useful to all off-roaders. It's meant to be essential reading, so don't leave it at home. If it doesn't help you to avoid trouble, it may help you to pass the time while you're waiting for help or, if the worst comes to the worst, you can always burn it and keep warm!

Considering that off-roaders seem to spend their entire lives getting muddy, it's a bit strange to suggest that cleanliness should be high on your list, but if you want your vehicle to perform efficiently and reliably then it certainly should be. Dirt is bad for your vehicle so after any off-road drive make sure you hose it down thoroughly, taking care to clean out underneath as well, because that's the area that needs it even if the vehicle's body doesn't look too bad. Hose under wheelarches and on the insides of the wheels around the hubs and brake fitments. Don't forget the engine, either; a dirty engine is the mark of a lazy off-roader and if that's you, then watch out. Dirt in the engine bay can turn to mud after a heavy dew, and that moisture can cause shorts in the electrics.

Hosing the engine down is simple as long as you remember to wrap up the distributor and air cleaner (where appropriate) in waterproof plastic bags and don't spray directly at fuse boxes and wiring.

It makes a lot of sense to actually waterproof your electrics. This sort of 'engine-proofing' is a simple DIY job. All you need is some all-purpose non-residue cleaner (the spray can variety is obviously the best), a proprietary ignition waterproofing spray and a silicone sealant.

Starting with the distributor, remove the cap and use the cleaner to remove all traces of dirt. When you're sure this has been done run a bead of sealant around the base of the cap, taking care not to leave any gaps, and replace. It should not be necessary, but if you are really worried you could then run a bead of silicone around the join on the outside of the cap. The golden rule with silicone sealer is that it can only be used once. When you next open the distributor, the sealant will be useless and must be replaced. It will peel off simply enough, but don't expect it to work twice.

You can also use the silicone sealant on bare wiring connections; a small blob here and there will work wonders. Many DIY mechanics

Even if you don't intend driving through rivers, your four-wheel drive will get wet. The battery terminals on this new Toyota don't just have fancy little covers; they also have a liberal coating of Vaseline. Check all the major electrical points and ensure that they are protected.

Failure to protect the engine will mean that it will get covered in mucky water. This four-wheel drive Bedford KB pick-up suffered terribly through poor driving technique – yet amazingly still kept running, though more by luck than judgment...

might be more used to using a blob of grease, which does the same job but attracts dirt and grit, not to mention being messy; silicone sealant is much cleaner.

Spray all ignition wires with the waterproofing agent and use the silicone sealant on the connections. Don't be afraid to pull back the rubber boots that cover these connections, then apply the sealant and push the boots back in place. If you thoroughly douse your engine in water those factory-fitted boots may not be enough. Some manufacturers are better than others at protecting their engines, so spend some time checking around yours, especially if it's secondhand. Replace any wiring that has a cracked or broken covering; this might be time consuming, but it costs very little and could save a lot. One of the best ways of protecting your engine from water is to learn how to drive through it — fording — properly. We deal with this elsewhere in the book.

If you are thinking of fitting extra lights to your off-roader take care to remember that the area directly under both front and rear bumpers is extremely vulnerable. Many of the top manufacturers fail to recognize this when fitting the extra poor-visibility rear light. So many times you see brand new four-wheel drives with this lamp fitted beneath the bumper. All this usually shows is that the driver doesn't take his vehicle off-road — because as soon as he does, that light will break. Remember that it is an offence if a rear light is so damaged that some white light is showing. Check that no wires are hanging down that could get caught as you drive over the rough. To those who want to fit front air dams with integral spotlights, we can only suggest that you make the whole unit easily detachable with the lights fitted with plugs because if you don't detach it before you go off-road then almost certainly the terrain will.

Underbody protection should have been carried out by the manufacturer, in other words where necessary skid plates will already have been fitted. These are usually fitted to protect the engine's sump and any exposed area near the gearbox/transfer case. Check where the guards are on your vehicle; they should be sufficient, but it is worth taking the time to have a look at them. If you have driven across a rocky surface and the skid plates have been hit they may have been dented or, worse still, split. A dent will have moved the plate closer to what it is supposed to be protecting; hit the same spot again and the damage could be much worse. Usually, skid plates are easy to remove so dents can be knocked out. For owners of four-wheel drive cars such as the Fiat Panda 4x4, for instance, it is worthwhile having a front skid plate fitted.

You can, of course, make your own protecting plates. If you do, think how it will work if you are stuck and want to reverse. Obviously you will turn up the front of the plate and allow it to skid over an obstruction, but remember that sometimes you will need to go backwards; if you have an open, flat, rear end to the plate it could dig into the mud and cause you more problems.

Wheels and tyres play an important part in the off-road experience and so it's worth looking after them. Should you keep the steel wheels that

You must remember that manufacturers, and more particularly their salesmen, are often not very switched-on off-roaders. High-intensity or reversing lights set below an off-roader's rear bumper will not last very long. Move them before you go off-road. Before, above: after, right...

are fitted to your vehicle or look for lighter alloy versions? Steel wheels are the type to stick with as they bend first rather than break. A bent wheel can be straightened with that hammer we told you to put in your tool kit. It's true that alloy wheels are lighter and therefore reduce the unsprung weight slightly, but it's not going to make that much difference.

Tyres, on the other hand, can make a great deal of difference and it's most important that you choose the right sort for the kind of driving you do. It's not very sensible to buy a good off-road tyre if you rarely take your vehicle off-road. A chunky tread might look good on the road but it's likely that your vehicle's on-road handling characteristics will deteriorate. This will be noticed in a 'wandering' feel when driving in a straight line and excessive weaving when braking, especially in the wet. These characteristics are particularly noticeable with the aggressive treads on many American brand tyres. Tyres with the more chunky tread patterns will wear out quicker if you spend a great deal of time on the road.

Tyre wear is very important as it will severely limit your off-road ability. It's no use waiting until the very last minute, or rather last millimetre, before changing the tyre. Worn tyres will be hopeless off-road where one of the major characteristics you should look for is how well a tyre 'self-cleans'; by that we mean how well a tyre rids itself of the

A good off-road tyre must be able to self-clean and you must be able to spot when it is worn. This picture shows two identical vehicles that have just driven up the same bank. The tyre on the left has been able to rid itself of much of the mud, while the tyre on the right (perhaps rather more worn) is still clogged with muck and therefore considerably less efficient.

porridge, or one of a number of proprietary products that you could consider keeping in your tool kit. The theory is that the foreign substance will find its way to the leak and plug the hole. Remember, though, if you are using any of these that the cooling system works under pressure, so in this case, just to get you home, relieve the pressure by releasing the radiator cap slightly before driving off, otherwise the pressure will continue to force the water out of the hole. Also, don't be tempted to chuck any old rubbish into your radiator; remember that you're going to have to flush it all out later and seal the leak properly.

If the temperature gauge starts to rise alarmingly but you can't see a leak it may be a much simpler problem. If you've been driving through either water or deep muddy puddles you may have thrown a lot of muck on to the front of the radiator and as you've driven along this will have become hot and baked itself on to the radiator matrix. A blast from a hose will release it, but of course that may not be possible out in the wilds. You can reduce the engine temperature considerably by running with the heater full on. It may be uncomfortable for the occupants, but it could save you a large repair bill.

With the sort of weather we get in Britain, it's likely that you'll have the heater on anyway because it'll be so cold! In ice and snow, good visibility is particularly important and you can keep the ice from your windscreen and stop the snow clinging to it by rubbing wet salt over the screen.

If you have to go out in your four-wheel drive in really bad weather we'd add a blanket and a flask of hot coffee as essentials. No matter what we say here, all too often four-wheel drivers suffer from moments of over exuberance and a belief that they won't get stuck. Some do. It helps if you can keep warm. It may also be of great assistance should you come across that Ford Sierra stuck in a ditch down some lonely country lane.

ADDITIONS TO YOUR MACHINE

Four-wheel drivers like to be different, and naturally they like to personalize their vehicles. You'll spend a great deal of time looking through magazines — especially *Off Road and 4 Wheel Drive*, of course — thinking about what you can buy to make your machine look different. This is obviously great fun, but care must be taken on a few points.

Lamp guards fitted front and rear not only look good, they also have the important quality of protecting your lights from damage off-road. Nudge bars at the front are probably the most popular off-road accessory. There are differing trains of thought about them, however, and some hardened off-roaders consider them to be more trouble than

Part of the trend in four-wheel drives has been the increasing scope for adding things to personalize your vehicle. That's great, but when fitting bull bars, for example, make sure they are properly attached, and remember that they do not make you invincible.

they are worth. Take great care to check where they are being fastened on your vehicle. Problems can occur should you hit something head-on; instead of some nasty but relatively straightforward bodywork repair, the impact force can be transmitted by the nudge bar to the mounting points on the chassis, which at worst could mean a damaged chassis as well. Never try to tow a vehicle by pulling on the bull bar as this will simply bend the brackets.

Side bars are also favoured by some people who want to make their vehicle look particularly tough. However, remember that they effectively lower your ground clearance, which could mean you are more likely to bottom out when crossing a ridge. So, no matter how great an accessory may look, always consider what effect it may have on the performance and versatility of your vehicle.

Such advice is especially true when it comes to engine modifications like turbocharging. There is a big business in turbocharging off-roaders but if that's what you want, please bear in mind what the turbo will do to your vehicle's performance off-road. Turbochargers give better on-road

A side bar is a smart addition to any machine, but fitting one like this will cut down your ground clearance.

performance and if you consider your vehicle to be a little sluggish they could be the answer. A number of companies offer turbocharging conversions on Suzuki SJs, for instance. If you want such a conversion on your Suzuki, make sure you drive a demonstrator *off-road* first. Problems can occur if such a conversion has a noticeable turbo lag — that's the time gap between the moment when you place your right foot hard down to get more power and that power actually arriving. This may not be such a problem on-road — just inconvenient — but off-road, when often you require immediate and delicate throttle contol, it can be a disaster.

The same goes for tampering with the suspension of an off-road vehicle. As they were designed to have long suspension travel for driving off-road, four-wheel drives do tend to lean rather a lot when cornered quickly on tarmac. The Range Rover is a typical example and some companies make handling kits for this model. These kits mainly consist of anti-roll bars that stop the vehicle rolling so much and thus also tend to reduce the suspension travel. Now one of the reasons why Land Rover themselves don't fit anti-roll bars to the Range Rover in the first place is because they believe they would reduce the vehicle's off-road abilities. They might well make your vehicle better to drive on the road, but can you accept a decrease in its performance off it?

There are numerous ways to increase the performance of your off-roader, in this case by adding a turbocharger to a Suzuki. Remember that while this will increase acceleration and top speed on the road it will also completely change the characteristics of the machine when you take it off-road.

If you have the choice between a bull bar, side bar or lamp guards... fit a sump guard instead. This may not be the most visually impressive addition to your machine, but if you are a serious off-roader, it's far more valuable.

There is a lot to be said for keeping the mechanical specification of a four-wheel drive vehicle the way that the manufacturer designed it — after all, they certainly should know what's best for that particular model. Meanwhile, a huge range of accessories are available that can enhance the enjoyment of your car without altering that delicate on-road/off-road balance. Happy shopping.

74

5

Driving off-road

Driving off-road is what owning a four-wheel drive is all about. Once you've tried it, you'll realize a number of things, the first being that it's not as difficult as perhaps you thought, but that it takes practice and experience to refine the techniques. You must also understand right from the start that you will never completely *master* off-road driving because each time you take to the hills there will be a different situation requiring a slightly different approach.

The first step is to go and watch others. As we have said elsewhere it pays to join a club. If you attend a club meeting or an off-road show you are bound to see some people driving badly, but you should also be reassured that off-roading is not some ancient mystic art known only to a select few. EVERYONE CAN DRIVE OFF-ROAD. And it's a very satisfying feeling crossing, climbing or descending an area of difficult terrain. Fundamentally you need to know your vehicle, to have it under your control with some sensitive use of the right foot and, where it is possible, to know the terrain on which you are driving.

Learning the vehicle may sound incredibly obvious, but you'd be surprised how many people don't! If your vehicle has selectable four-wheel drive make sure you know how it is engaged. If your vehicle has free-wheeling front hubs, then always have those locked before you move off towards the tricky stuff. Without the free-wheeling hubs engaged, moving the transfer box lever from two to four-wheel drive will not help you at all — you will merely be turning the front prop shaft and drive shafts but not the front wheels (for a more detailed explanation of the workings of free-wheeling hubs turn back to the section *Mind your language*). If you have automatic front hubs four-wheel drive selection is simply a case of slipping the transfer box lever into the correct position. Is your vehicle fitted with differential locks? Make sure you understand

Low ratio, second gear and progressive use of the throttle will get you up a slippery slope like this without the dreaded wheelspin.

this before you go off-road. If you have a Land Rover or Range Rover make sure the centre diff is locked just as you start the rough stuff, and remember to disengage it when on firm ground.

Wherever you go, you can guarantee it's going to be bumpy, so ensure that both you and your passengers are ready for it. Seat belts should be worn despite the fact that if you are on private land the front seat belt law doesn't apply. Tell your passengers to have a firm hand hold to steady themselves; many vehicles have door straps and a useful hand hold on the facia.

You'll find that the steering wheel appears to have a mind of its own when off-road, but don't fight it by hanging on for dear life; it's often a case of guiding rather than steering. Keep those thumbs outside the steering wheel rim as there will be occasions when a severe kickback from the front wheels hitting an obstacle will cause the wheel to spin violently; if you've got a thumb in there, it can be painful.

The vast majority of off-roading is done with the vehicle in Low range

Not like this! Keep those thumbs out of the way. When off-road the steering wheel will sometimes have a mind or its own and spin violently. It's very painful if you've got a thumb in the way.

Coming down, keep those feet out of it, too. Believe it or not, your vehicle will be in control going down hill with your feet out of the way. Some would prefer to see the right foot hovering over the throttle, but never have your left foot near the clutch. You do not want to declutch...

Coming down is even more fun then going up. Let the vehicle do most of the work; low ratio, first gear, feet off everything. If the back starts to slide, a delicate amount of throttle will straighten things up.

(full explanation of the transfer box is in the *Mind your language* section). There will be times when you will be off-road and in four-wheel drive High, but in such situations the going will obviously be easy. It's your ability to slip into Low range that makes off-roading possible. It increases the torque to the wheels and allows you to go much slower than you thought possible without having to slip the clutch. You never slip the clutch off-road — if you do, you are in the wrong gear and more likely to get into trouble.

Is there a golden rule in off-roading? That's the sort of question that will keep a good pub argument going for hours. This author's contribution to the debate is that the single most important thing to remember is 'Take it easy'. It is always a case of brain being able to go where brawn will simply get you large repair bills. The skill in driving off-road comes from subtle use of the right pedal, very little use of the middle one, while the clutch is either in or out — no half measures. If you think it's a case of white-knuckled, wheel-spinning, red mist in front of the eyes, where speed is the only thing that will get you through, then stop reading this now and go away. You're wrong. The best off-roaders drive 10 to 15 yards ahead; they are reading the ground to see what is coming up next, planning where to direct the vehicle. Often, quite often in fact, that will mean stopping the vehicle, getting out and having a look. This isn't the reaction of some limp-wristed wimp, it is the action of an intelligent driver who stands a far better chance of not getting stuck.

At the top of a hill, ease off gently as you hit the crest – too much throttle will see you leap over the lip (above); it may look dramatic but it is not advisable. Below: always approach a descent square-on; never try to emulate this driver, who is attacking at an angle. A mistake like this could see you roll over.

We obviously can't explain here exactly what gear you should be in, and when, but we will try and get you into the right frame of mind by explaining the basics. One major rule that always applies is never to spin the wheels if it is not necessary. Spinning wheels do not mean you are going fast — usually it is quite the opposite — but more important, you could be 'digging in', actually making deeper ruts and lowering the vehicle into the ground.

If you are just driving straight ahead off-road, it's unlikely that you will want first gear Low range. Second and third are the gears most frequently used — which reduces the risk of wheelspin — although it is obviously difficult to be dogmatic because it depends on the vehicle you are driving and where. You will not necessarily need first gear even to pull away; try it in second, which will cut out one gear change and allow you to concentrate on driving smoothly.

Gentle, easy movements are called for with both the throttle and the steering wheel. Plant your right foot down hard in soft ground and the wheels will spin. Yank the steering wheel hard one way and you will plough straight on. So take it nice and easy.

Hills and off-roaders are always attracted to one another like magic. If there's a hill you'll want to climb it. Always approach a hill as directly as possible; don't climb at an angle because you are asking for trouble and a potential roll-over. Look carefully at the angle at the bottom. If it's a gentle rise then you can put on the power and accelerate gradually, with more and more power being fed in as needed. Don't overdo it, as you will want to ease off at the top — rather than brake severely. If the angle of the hill or obstacle is more severe you should get those front wheels up the base of the hill before you start to pile on the power. If you fly at the obstacle the sharp angle could send your front wheels jumping off the ground, and that's exactly what you don't want. Don't worry if you fail to make it to the top; if you got up you can get down again and have another go — don't panic as your momentum slows down and you to come to a halt because it's not a problem.

When you come to a halt, apply the handbrake. Now, do you know your vehicle? Does the handbrake work on the transmission or the wheels? If it's a transmission brake (Land Rovers, Range Rovers and Suzukis) then you have effectively locked all four wheels, but wait until you are stationary before pulling it on to avoid unnecessary jolting of the transmission. Also, pull the handbrake on gently, don't just yank it on against all the rachet. If your handbrake is just to the wheels, pull it on and, once the engine has stopped, put the vehicle into gear. Now you have time to access the situation. Your four-wheel drive Low ratio also works in reverse, of course, so let's go back down and try again. *Never* try to turn the vehicle around and drive down forwards. A vehicle sideways

Look before you leap... This is not the action of a coward, just a sensible off-roader who wants to know what's over the edge when he can't see from the driver's seat.

across a slope is in danger of rolling. Some people may say that there are times when you might be able to do this, but for safety's sake *never* is the best policy. With the engine off, select reverse, foot completely off the clutch and right foot off the throttle, start the engine and release the handbrake. You will instantly get superb engine braking and with the Low ratio you will be able to trickle down the hill following the route you came up. Don't brake and for pity's sake don't declutch. If a rolling reverse start like that seems too difficult, then start the car normally, holding it on the foot brake, engage reverse and release the brake — you will not go careering down the hill backwards out of control if you are in Low ratio reverse with your feet off everything.

This writer believes that going down hills safely is the most impressive ability that a four-wheel drive can demonstrate, and long descents will certainly most impress your passengers, especially if they are new to off-roading. They'll think you are such a good driver and we bet you won't tell them that it's easy and has little driver input! Quite simply, going forwards as well as reversing, you let the vehicle do the work. Often you will not be able to see all the way down a hill from the cab, so stop, put the handbrake on, step out and have a look. Set the vehicle up so that it

Remember that on the road four-wheel drives have such long suspension travel that severe cornering will be alarming. This photograph has a professional driving instructor pushing a Land Rover to its limits – look at the distortion of that front tyre.

Soft surfaces like sand can be a problem. This driver has just been caught by an innocent looking ridge which has made the front wheels useless and allowed the rear wheels to spin themselves into a deep hole. Much spade work was necessary here.

is at right angles to the edge; you should aim to go straight down wherever possible, not at an angle. Engage Low ratio first gear, then stick both your feet behind your neck! OK, so that's a bit uncomfortable, but just don't touch any of the pedals. On most occasions the engine's braking ability will see you chug down under complete control without actually doing anything but steer gently.

Obviously, there are hills and hills. If you do feel the speed is too rapid then gentle applications of the brake can be made, but we mean gentle and it is important not to lock the wheels because if you do, you will slide and be out of control. *Never* disengage the clutch because doing so will remove drive and you will no longer be in control — you'll be in trouble. If as you descend you feel the rear of the vehicle stepping out of line and you are beginning to slide sideways, accelerate a little. Now this is very easy to write but never very easy to do at first, but it gives you the grip to allow you to straighten up, lift off and go down in the correct direction.

The Low range engine braking capabilities that make slow secure downhill descents possible are underlined by those vehicles that have diesel power units. The high compression of the diesel engine will almost stop the vehicle dead in its tracks when it is going down some descents. However, sometimes it is necessary to make allowances for this. If the conditions are particularly slippery and the descent very steep, the engine braking of a diesel in first gear Low range will be similar to putting the brake hard on. The wheels will be turning so slowly that they may actually 'toboggan' down the hill. In such a situation second gear Low range could be better as this will keep the wheels turning without sliding.

When driving along the straight and narrow remember how much ground clearance you have under your vehicle. If you straddle rocks or tree stumps are they likely to hit your differentials?

If you are driving along a well used lane, it's likely that you will be driving in ruts. Sometimes this will be a little like driving a vehicle on rails; you won't need to steer, the grooves in the ground will direct you along. This assumes, of course, that you want to go in the direction of the ruts! If you want to go in a different direction, try to keep out of the ruts because once you are in them it can sometimes be difficult to get out again. Be careful not to put too much lock on against the ruts while momentum keeps ploughing you along because if your front wheels suddenly find some grip from a rock or a firmer piece of ground you could find yourself lurching in the direction of the front wheels but not necessarily in the direction you want to go. Read the ground carefully to find somewhere where you can drive up and out of deep ruts, and always remember where those front wheels are pointing.

These really are the basics of off-road driving. Next, we offer specific advice regarding different surfaces, but basically if you take care along the lines explained above and add a little experience, you'll soon get the hang of it. We guarantee you'll love it.

In Britain, you will find that much of your off-roading will be done on mud — and it will be wet. Of course, mud comes in all different types and only experience will really help here. Remember that mud will fill in the grooves of your tyres and if they have limited self-cleaning ability their grip will be diminished. Off-roaders don't get far with worn tyres! The mud will also collect on the outside of the tyre around the wheel, so

Never attempt to traverse a slope if you get stuck going up. It's much better to come down backwards than try to turn round as if you are in Tesco's car park. This Mercedes-Benz is on the verge of rolling over and the driver, who has got out, has a real problem. Look at that rear wheel.

watch out for this and stop and clean it off where necessary. If the going ahead looks particularly nasty get out and see how firm it is under the surface — just because there are other tyre tracks it doesn't mean it's safe for you to follow them. Wet mud is the best medium for getting stuck, and that's when you will be pleased if you have fitted a winch, as we explain later in this chapter.

You're less likely to be driving on rocks in the UK, but if you do, take care. They can cause a great deal of expensive damage for the careless driver. Over routes that have particularly large rocks you must carefully select the rocks that can be safely straddled without causing any damage to the underside of your vehicle.

Unless you go down to a beach, you are not likely to encounter much sand in the UK. We don't have the opportunity to drive across vast desert expanses as, for instance, off-roaders do in America. Perhaps that's a good thing, because sand is one of the most difficult surfaces to cross and probably the easiest in which to get stuck. If you use too much right foot, the wheelspin will quickly bury you in the sand, but if you have insufficient momentum, the slightest rise in the land — for example when crossing a small dune — will defeat you and bring you to a standstill. Obviously there are special tyres designed for sand, but that's an expensive way of solving the situation. Tyres do, however, provide part of the answer. You must let the tyre pressures down to soften the tyre and allow the weight of the vehicle to spread more of the tyre over the sand to give it a larger contact area. In this respect it's the exact opposite to mud and snow, where smaller-section, thinner tyres are the best bet and large, fat tyres a disadvantage.

Not too fast, but steady and constant, is the best bet if you have to negotiate sand, but we stress that this is not a suitable medium for the absolute beginner to try. If and when you do, make sure you have another vehicle (or a winch) to pull you out when you get stuck.

It's much more likely that you will find yourself driving on snow and ice. This is where the four-wheel drive owner finds he has the enviable ability to go where others can't — often just on main roads! For one or two weeks every year, some major roads in mainland Britain become impassable, except for off-roaders; the problem comes when some four-wheel drivers think that they are invincible. The golden rule when driving on snow and ice is to remember that although you will have the traction to go where others are slipping and sliding, you don't have any better method of stopping because the laws of gravity and motion apply to 4x4s as well. As with any vehicle on snow and ice, cadence braking is called for; your foot goes on and off the brake, taking it off just before the wheel locks, then reapplying it. This is the human equivalent to ABS braking, which owners of some 4x4 cars, including Sierra, Audi and

BMW, are lucky enough to have fitted as standard. We all have it fitted if we use our brains, however. The idea is not to lock the wheels because a locked wheel will not steer, whereas a turning one will.

Always use four-wheel drive when there's snow about and remember that many of the off-road rules apply when driving on the road; the most important one is to avoid wheelspin. Pull away in second, or even third if it's really slippery.

When the weather is really bad, remember to have that tow rope, a warm blanket and preferably a flask of hot coffee or tea with you. You may not need it, but there's a good chance that you may end up pulling some poor two-wheel driver out of a ditch and he, or she, will be very grateful.

This is how *not* to drive through water. Too fast and you'll drown the engine. It may look spectacular, but really it's the action of an idiot.

The final piece of driving advice is not about driving on, but driving through. Four-wheel drives quite like driving through water, and if done properly you shouldn't get your feet or anything else wet. We have explained how to waterproof your vehicle elsewhere, in *Tricks of the trade*, but even those suggestions won't save you from flooding the engine if you drive badly. The main thing to avoid is too much water in the engine bay, too soon. If you have a large rubber floor mat in the vehicle, fix it across the front of the radiator grille (trapping it under the bonnet often works). What you must avoid most of all is water into the air filter as it could then find its way into the engine.

First have a good look at where you hope to drive. Either wade into the stream or river, or take a stick and check both how deep the water is and

Not bad, but still a little too enthusiastic. The initial contact with the water is the difficult bit. You do not want too much of a splash, but you need to go fast enough to keep the momentum going.

how firm the base. Don't just prod aimlessly about in the water, look for where any previous wheel tracks might be as it will obviously be much deeper there.

Once you're ready to go through, make sure that all the doors are shut and ease yourself into the water. This may well mean that you need first gear Low ratio to get down a bank, so take it easy. You are trying to avoid a big bow wave that could break over the bonnet — that would be bad driving. Keep a constant but easy pace and it will probably pay to slip from first to Low ratio second gear once on the level as this will give you a better gear for climbing out the other side. As you are climbing a bank, more power can be fed in as you start to rise out of the water. If you do get stuck, keep the engine running as this will stop water going the wrong way up the exhaust pipe, and remember to climb out of the window and not to open the door. If you are stranded, it may be possible to reverse (you should be able to drive out the way you went in if you're careful) and then you can try again. If, on the other hand, you're very stuck in the middle of it all, we hope you've either got a winch fitted (they work under water) or a friend is close by with another vehicle on terra firma.

When it comes to off-roading, the ability to know how to winch is second only to your ability to drive. Indeed, if you know how to winch properly, it may save you from situations into which your driving has dropped you! That's obviously a little unfair because anyone who has done any form of even mildly serious off-roading will know that a winch is often the *only* way through, irrespective to how good the driver may be. So it's important to know how to use a winch properly.

There are two major types of winches; electric and mechanical. The electrically-operated winches are the most popular for the off-road enthusiast, the wire cable being operated from the vehicle's battery using a hand-held remote control. The mechanical winch has the same wire cable on a drum, but is driven by the engine and controlled using the vehicle's accelerator pedal.

Winching is often great fun, but it is always potentially dangerous. What, then, are the techniques involved to enable you to winch successfully? There's certainly no great mystique about it, despite what some people may imply. Everyone can become a good winch technician, and that's not something you can say about driving, despite what some instructors may suggest. Follow some basic rules, use common sense, always be aware of the potential danger, pick up some tips from the experts and you should be able to get out of most sticky situations.

There are an impressive number of winches on the market. For the off-roader who just wants to pull his own or another standard four-wheel drive, or perhaps pull a boat out of water, a winch with a pulling capacity of 8,000lb is sufficient. Winches with a pulling power of 10,000 or

Too much speed down a slope into a water splash and you will get wet – and it's not necessary.

Perfect, and in very deep water, too. The momentum is there to keep the bow wave in front of the vehicle, but it's not going over the bonnet at all.

When using a winch, always use strong gloves when handling the winch cable.

12,000lb are available, but are really intended for commercial and industrial use. After that, you need some standard accessories and the equipment that we will detail here and you're ready.

The remote-control nature of winching means that it is actually possible to do the job on your own, but we advise against it. Obviously, some people drive 4x4s for a living, are often alone and therefore have no choice, but those of us who go off-road for pleasure have the choice and we say you must take someone with you. Ideally you should always travel with another vehicle (this should be a golden rule if you don't have a winch fitted), but even if travelling in a solo vehicle, a partner, a winch and the right sort of accessories should see you through. Two people is the ideal number and you should agree from the start who is doing what. For our purposes, we will call one the operator and the other the assistant.

As the title suggests, the operator is in sole charge of the winch via the hand control. Always unwind all of the control's wire before connecting to the winch; this gives you the chance to check for any fraying or breaks in the casing. There's a good 6ft or so of this wire, so if you are not careful it will get tangled round something, possibly even the wheels. Once plugged in, wind it around the driver's door mirror and lay the control on the bonnet or through the open driver's door window on to the facia. Never have the control in your hand while anyone's fingers are near the winch; your assistant should always see where the control is before he, or she, gets useful fingers anywhere near the wire cable on the drum.

You must decide on the anchoring point you intend to use before you get out all the equipment. Ideally you want a solid anchorage point, dead centre to the front of the vehicle, *i.e.* directly ahead of the winch. Obviously, this is not always possible, and a small angle is not a problem. A good solid tree is the most likely point. Always check to see that it has leaves or buds on it to ensure that it is not dead — even thick trees will be pulled straight down by an 8,000lb winch if they are dead. If a fully grown tree is not available, a group of small trees or saplings will do. The assistant will put the winching strap around this anchorage point. If you are going to winch regularly buy a proper strap. It is possible to use a good strong rope with properly fitted hooks on each end, but never wind the wire cable around a tree and hook it back onto itself; this is extremely damaging to the tree and potentially dangerous to you as it could simply cut through the tree and then whiplash back towards the vehicle.

Once you have decided where it will be secured, check the ground over which the cable will travel. Take care, if you can see that it will touch the ground, that there are no sharp rocks or protrusions that could damage the cable. If you are at all unsure, dig a small trench to act as a gully for the cable to pull through, or use a log as a fulcrum over which the cable can run.

There are two ways of unwinding the winch cable, the easy and the hard. The easy way is to spool the wire out using the winch motor. If you do this, just bear in mind that you are using the vehicle's battery and it is this component that is very important to you; if you flatten it and you are on your own, you could be in big trouble. If, therefore, you know that you are going to be doing a lot of winching, engage the winch's freewheel and physically pull the cable out. Always wear a pair of strong gloves, preferably thick leather ones; *never* touch the cable with bare hands.

As the assistant is paying out the line, the operator can use the opportunity to examine the cable as it is unravelled. While the assistant is securing it to the chosen anchorage point, the operator must maintain the tension on the cable that is still wound on the drum. If the cable is allowed to go slack on the drum, when you switch on to winch it will not wind itself neatly on to the drum and that can be disastrous. If you are

Winch and drive. The driver has control of the winch in this situation, but his assistant is helping to instruct him on what to do and when it looks possible to simply drive.

paying out the maximum amount of line, always ensure that you keep a minimum of four turns of cable around the drum. The operator now waits for the assistant to indicate that all is secure at his end. This is the point at which you will start using your own sign language.

With the engine running and the likelihood that you are several yards apart, shouting instructions is of little use. Agree a code between you beforehand. A good code is to make a 'biting' movement between the fingers and thumb of one hand to indicate a single blip on the hand control. 'Biting' in rapid succession means keep the finger on the button. You also need to know when your assistant wants you to pay out the line or pull it in, and most importantly you need to know when he means *stop*.

Take up the slack, stop and check that everything is still OK. Be sure the cable is winding nicely on the drum, check that all anchorage points are secure. You are now ready to start winching.

At this point you, the operator, will discover that you are on the wrong side of the cable, for sure. The shortest route to where you want to be is a quick step over the taut wire. *Don't.* Never step over the cable under tension; it may seem a real pain to walk around the vehicle, but it is a lot better than the pain of slipping and causing the taut cable to break or become detached. The operator's position during winching has to be the safest possible; often he will want to be behind the wheel if he intends winching and driving, or to the side of the vehicle out of the way of the cable should a disaster occur and the line break.

Winching a vehicle is very satisfying. The power of these little winches is very impressive when one is used to extricate a stricken four-wheel drive from some bottomless bog. Control in hand, you can just heave the vehicle out, taking care to watch that the line is winding properly on to the drum. Once again, however, we are talking about battery life and the possibility that the winch may need a little help. In this case it will be necessary to winch and drive.

Winching and driving does take a little practice. The idea is to drive when you have grip and winch when you haven't. The important thing is that it's a case of clutch either in or out, no half measures. Don't slip it. Not only will winching and driving help save the battery, you will also find out sooner when you have the grip to continue driving. To winch and drive effectively calls for a piece of team-work and you will need your assistant alongside shouting instructions, probably through the open passenger door window as he or she will have a better view of the cable.

After a successful recovery, paying the cable back on to the drum means the same care must be taken as before, keeping it under tension so that it winds on firmly. The danger point here comes right at the end when you only have a short length of cable and it needs securing. Every operator must know how his, or her, winch works, and by that we mean when you release the switch you must know how much cable continues to be payed in during the motor's 'over-run'. Carelessness here could lead to lost fingers.

Besides the winch, tree strap, good strong rope with professionally attached hooks on each end and a good stout pair of gloves, the other major piece of equipment you should carry is a snatch block. This is a simple pulley that can be clipped over the wire cable to double up the pulling power of your winch.

By this we mean that the cable can come from the winch to the anchorage point, around the snatch block wheel and then back to the vehicle, where it is firmly attached to a towing eye. The snatch block is attached to your anchorage point. Doing this gives you a mechanical advantage of 2:1, in other words, if you have an 8,000lb winch, doubling up like this by using a snatch block gives you 16,000lb of pulling power. The snatch block also allows you more flexibility when it comes to choosing your anchorage point, as you can see from the accompanying photographs.

There will be times when there are just no suitable places for you to attach your winch. In these cases it's time to find a ground anchor. It may

Ready to go off-roading? Then know where you have stowed all your gear. This photograph has been posed, but don't just chuck all your gear in the back. You may need it in a hurry and it may be dark, so make sure you know where everything is located.

be that you have two vehicles and the one which is stuck doesn't have the winch. If, therefore, you simply attempt to pull it out with a stationary recovery vehicle, you stand just as much chance of pulling the safe vehicle towards the stranded one. It may be necessary to secure the rear of the winching vehicle to a tree with a tow rope, or wedge the vehicle up against a tree. You can also use sturdy wheel ground anchors. With these you simply drive the recovery vehicle on to them and the weight of the vehicle embeds them firmly into the ground and makes it impossible for the vehicle to slide across the mud when winching. To recover them when you've finished, all you do is hook the chains over the bumper and reverse. They are effective, but rather bulky for the weekend off-roader to have permanently aboard his vehicle. Proprietary ground anchors are available; however, they are not cheap for the weekend man and more often they are used commercially.

If you are on your own, treeless, and don't have a proprietary ground anchor, then it's time to use the age old trick of the spare wheel. Basically, you bury the vehicle's spare wheel in the ground with the winch cable attached and haul yourself out. It is hard work and messy, but very effective!

So, if you've read, understood and inwardly digested all the above advice about driving off-road, what are you waiting for? Go and have some fun!

6

Where can I drive?

As the proud owner of a four-wheel drive, it's natural to want to charge off into the country, turn off the main road and head for the hills. Please don't, at least not until you've read this chapter. Green laning is one of the major pleasures of running a four-wheel drive, but it can also be a big problem if you are not careful. There are some golden rules that must not be broken.

To start at the beginning, there's no legal definition of a green lane or a green road, so don't go looking for them on a map. It's merely a description of a track that does not have a metalled surface — brown laning would be a more accurate term when you consider most of them are muddy, but it doesn't have quite the same ring to it, does it? What you need to know *before* you drive along any green lane is whether it has vehicular Rights of Way. Just because you can see the tyre marks of other vehicles does not mean it's open to the public.

All Rights of Way information is recorded on definitive maps that are held by the respective highway authorities. This usually means visiting your local county council — don't worry, these maps are available for inspection by the public. They will show all tracks, footpaths, bridleways and 'roads used as public paths'; these are the ones you are interested in, but a word of caution – not all RUPPs have vehicular rights. As a rough rule of thumb, only about one RUPP in five carries vehicular rights, so it's not worth the gamble. RUPPs are constantly under review to establish their classification and what you are looking for are tracks classified as BOATs, 'byways open to all traffic'. A BOAT is a highway over which the public have right of way whether travelling on foot, on horseback, or in a four-wheel drive. A number of BOATs have Traffic Regulation Orders made on them to restrict vehicular rights on part of the route, or for particular types of traffic, so take care to note if that is the case.

You must learn to read and understand maps. The author poses for the camera before going off down some of the lovely green lanes in Wales. We say 'poses' because he had a local guide in the lead vehicle...

You cannot, therefore, just go out and buy an Ordnance Survey map, check where the RUPPs are, and drive down them happy in the knowledge that you have Rights of Way. Also, some editions of the OS map don't distinguish between RUPPs and BOATs, so look at the symbols very carefully.

There are two ways to tackle the problem of which green lanes you can drive. You may live in an area where there is a particular green lane along which you would like to be able to drive. It should be relatively simple to check with your local council the status of that route and others in your area. The attitude of councils about four-wheel drivers does vary. Be polite, but be firm; don't let them fob you off. With some councils this whole problem is one which they seem reluctant to deal with, so you'll have to persevere. If that seems to be too daunting a task on your own, fear not, there is an answer; join a club. In the following section we detail the different four-wheel drive clubs and list all their addresses, so there's likely to be one near you. Contact your local club and ask if they have a Rights of Way Officer. Most of the clubs have such a post and these

One of the Golden Rules when going green laning is not to go alone. Two is not only more fun, it's far safer.

people are the experts, especially about local problems. In simple terms they should be able to tell you where you can and cannot drive. Some of the top clubs have joined a new organization called the Land Access and Rights Association. LARA has been formed to put the case of the motorist, including green laning, to the authorities.

Once a member of a club, you will learn a lot about the legal problems concerning green laning. That knowledge will mean you are far better armed to contact your local council. The information that you collect can then be fed back to the club for the benefit of others.

GREEN LANING: THE RULES

Hopefully, all the above problems will not put you off going green laning. They certainly weren't intended to, and when you have enjoyed a run through the countryside in your four-wheel drive, you'll agree it was worth all the effort.

Once on the green lane, there are some more golden rules that all four-wheel drivers should adhere to:

It is not a race, so drive slowly. Keep the vehicle in second or third gear Low ratio; if you are in High ratio, you're probably driving a bit too quickly. Remember that other people have a right to the track as well. Whenever possible, stop for pedestrians and horses. It's often here that you will need all your patience. Unfortunately, a few off-roaders are giving the majority a bad name, and this is ammunition to the members of the Ramblers Association who would like to see all vehicles banned from all green lanes. Don't help their cause, they are strong enough as it is. The Ramblers Association have well over 50,000 paid-up members, a number of full-time staff, are situated just around the corner from Parliament and have MPs as officers of the association. Enough said?

You may also meet the farmer or landowner through whose land you are driving. Stop and explain your presence politely. Hopefully you will be armed with the information that confirms vehicular Rights of Way down this track. Report all such meetings back to your club and to the relative highway authority.

You may also meet a more concrete obstruction in the form of a fence. Even if you are absolutely convinced that it shouldn't be there, don't remove it yourself. Report it to the council; if the Rights of Way exist for this track, it's the council's duty to remove such obstructions. If a tree or large bush has fallen across the path you are at liberty to move it, but you can't take the wood home as it belongs to the land owner.

Joining a club will mean that you will probably go green laning in groups. It's best to keep these to small manageable numbers; 50 or so vehicles can look like something of an invasion!

It may seem like common sense, but some people don't seem to have any, so remember:
SHUT GATES AFTER YOU!

This is one authorized green lane that goes through farmland. If he'll shoot dogs, don't think he'll smile sweetly if you act the goat. Actually, 10 minutes after this picture was taken we met him, and he liked sensible off-roaders and told us to come back.

If you are following a route and become unsure of exactly where it goes next, get out and walk. If you still can't make out where the track goes, the safest bet is to go back the way you came. Always keep a record of your green laning runs, where you go and when. Quite often tracks come under road closure orders and your notes could be used as evidence that the route is used regularly and therefore should be kept open.

This all seems rather like the preaching of a cynical old school teacher. The problem is that although there are some 120,000 miles of non-

When you go off-road, you'll get a puncture and it will be raining... it always is when you get a puncture, so be prepared!

metalled tracks throughout the UK, they are under threat. Many of them are being used perfectly sensibly by off-roaders and many more could be. There is a growing movement against green laning which is now facing the growing enthusiasm for four-wheel drive vehicles. If all off-road enthusiasts act sensibly, we are a potent force against having these historically significant routes closed *forever*; once a route is closed it will never be opened again.

The Countryside Commission are backing a plan to have all the non-road tracks reclassified. As this is being written, the four-wheel drive enthusiast is reeling from a report from the National Society for Nature Conservation saying that off-roaders are destroying the nation's wildlife. Looked at in detail, the report highlights 130 cases of damage caused by off-roaders; take that further and you find that only 23 of those cases were by four-wheel drives (the remainder were from motorcycles). National newspaper coverage is calling *you* a hooligan on the basis of 23 instances over 120,000 miles of track . . .

The answer is to join a club, get the support necessary and enjoy the delights of green laning. Don't worry, it is worth the effort, that's for sure.

A four-wheel drive will take you to some amazing places. This picture shows an Isuzu Trooper driven by the author somewhere in the Italian Alps. If you think it looks good in the picture, we can assure you that it's even more fantastic from behind the wheel. This is what makes four-wheel drive special.

7

Learning in good company

Safe but effective off-road driving employs techniques unknown to ordinary motorists. Newcomers — and long-time 4×4 owners who rarely venture off the tarmac – can benefit from expert tuition, and in recent years a number of off-road driving schools and courses have been developed. Prominent among them is the Overlander off-road centre at East Foldhay, near Crediton in the heart of Devon, conducted by David Bowyer and co-instructor Keith Hart.

Even an experienced off-roader can find a well-organized training session valuable. Ross Floyd has owned a Land Rover for nine years, runs the marque's Series II Club, and thought that he had little to learn about motoring in the rough. He signed up for a weekend course at David Bowyer's school and found it illuminating – as well as fun.

* * *

There were six of us, with four vehicles: a police officer and his wife with a brand-new Land Rover Diesel Turbo County, a computer specialist with a Series II Land Rover, a doctor with a Fiat Panda 4×4, and my wife Gill and I with our restored and just resprayed Series II.

The course starts in the classroom adjoining the Overlander office. Keith Hart ploughed straight into the principles of off-roading, described in a simple and easy-to-follow way, and left plenty of time for questions. The lecture covered subjects as diverse as vehicle preparation, descending and ascending, departure angles, engine braking, crossing ditches, going through gullies, driving along rough tracks, traversing hills, slopes, and wading.

Introduction over, we moved outside to the vehicles. Each had a thorough look over to ensure that there was nothing loose or missing, all equipment was stowed securely, batteries were clamped, wading plugs

Ready to go: freewheel hubs locked, spare wheel removed from the bonnet and wing mirrors out of harm's way.

fitted, and the distributor had a waterproofing smear of silicone grease. The spare wheel had to be removed from the bonnet of my Land Rover to improve forward visibility and the tow hook had to be raised for greater clearance at the rear, allowing increased departure angle. All of us were told to decrease tyre pressure to around 20psi — it was going to be muddy!

Time to get out on the course. With freewheel hubs firmly locked, we followed David Bowyer's Range Rover out through the 'jungle' section to the starting point. Keith followed in his Series I Land Rover.

All was then revealed. The track has been dug into the hillside and across the valley and contains just about everything that an off-road driver might encounter — or hope to find. It is completely non-damaging and some clever ideas have been incorporated to prevent underbody and panel damage. There are humps, gullies, slopes, ditches, railway sleepers, a shingle bed, a log crossing, even a miniature quarry and artificial stream bed. There is a bog, too, and a super section of river for deep wading practice. Most daunting of all is a 45-degree bank.

We lined up in front of the first main obstacle. David and Keith were to team up with each of us in turn. Keith jumped into the passenger seat

Series II Land Rovers in procession over the tyre hump, one of the ingeniously contrived non-damaging obstacles at the Overlander centre.

of my Land Rover, while David passengered the vehicle in front. We watched them go over the first tyre hump and along a side slope. I followed, Keith advising all the way about which gear to use, the right approach angle and so on. After another two or three obstacles, weaving around cane poles set in rough terrain, straddling ruts, and climbing to the top of the hill through a pot-holed gulley, we stopped at the quarry.

It was interesting to observe the progress of others through the various obstacles. The Panda, not surprisingly, needed a different line of approach to the Land Rovers, but it got through with no difficulty.

Our instructors then explained the correct way to tackle the three steep descents that confronted us — with two cross-ditches and a short, sharp hump thrown in for good measure. We were all rather flabbergasted, looking down the first stony, twisting gulley and then the 45-degree bank into the hole below.

It was soon my turn to try them. Bringing the vehicle to the top of the gulley, head out of the window trying to see where the track went, the instructions were, 'As you move over the edge, FEET OFF EVERYTHING! All you have to do is steer. KEEP YOUR THUMBS OUT.' With no drama we made it to the bottom of the valley. Some of the excitement — and the confidence — of my early 'wild' Land Rover days began to return.

We tackled the remainder of the course in the same way, with the instructors ensuring that we negotiated each obstacle in the correct way

— in the right gear and at the right speed. The route back to the high ground of the car park took us through wash-outs and watercourses down by the river.

After lunch at a nearby inn, it was Gill's turn to take the driving seat. Mid-afternoon, after the ladies had almost an hour of personal tuition, we stopped for a brief discussion and then moved on to individual training on three other sections not previously used.

First, we were taught the art of safely bringing our vehicles down a hillside backwards after stalling or running out of grip near the top. Disconcerting at first, it is easy when the correct technique is mastered. Then we were shown how to tackle a very deep 'vee' gulley with an instructor in front directing where to steer. Finally, we were taught to negotiate a deep gulley with a 50-foot climb beyond it.

A last word of advice before tackling the 45-degree bank. Over 1,400 trees and shrubs have subsequently been planted to re-integrate David Bowyer's land-scaped course into the peaceful Devon country-side of its surroundings.

'Let's see what you've all learnt', said David, introducing us to the trials section. First we walked the course, comprising 10 'gates' (marker canes) set out to form a dozen obstacles. I think that we all realized that it was best to select second gear in low ratio and drive on the throttle. 'You are learning fast', David encouraged. 'Now turn round and tackle it in the reverse direction!' That put a new perspective on it . . . but we all made it without incident.

Keith then suggested that we did a green road run. Well, not exactly — our task was to negotiate the whole course in the opposite direction. There would be no signs to follow and approaches would be quite different. And what about that 45-degree bank? Led by the Land Rover Ninety (with the Panda joining in only for the easier sections), the 45-degree climb was tackled with ease, David and Keith sitting in with us to ensure that we used the right gear and right speed (low second, flat out); with some scrabbling for grip and a windscreen full of blue Devon sky we went over the top,

It was 6 o'clock and time to go back to the classroom. Whilst Keith made the tea, David set up the video and a specially-made film covering all aspects of off-road driving. It served as a timely reminder of the many things we had learned during the day.

After a peaceful night at a local hotel, day two started with a session on winching techniques. Keith's introductory lecture included the basics of using electric drum winches, the mechanical capstan type and various hand winches. He emphasized how important it is to have a winch fitted when venturing into unknown territory. He also made it clear that green roading is something that should be done in groups. The use of ground anchors, strops, ropes and snatches and high-lift jacks was also covered.

We took a high-lift jack out to the car park for a demonstration. Using the towing point of his Land Rover, Keith was able to raise it with ease. He then showed how to use it to lift a stuck vehicle sideways out of a rut.

Next was the use of a capstan winch, demonstrated on David's Series I Land Rover. Our 'load' was the course Range Rover on the end of the winch rope on a mild slope. I have a similar capstan winch and have always used manilla rope. This exercise showed me how much better a purpose-made winching rope is for control of recovery by pulling, holding and lowering.

Then it was into the mire. We were told to walk the winching section to establish the best route. The Panda went into the mud-hole first and made it to the other side. With the canes narrowed for the Land Rover, it was my turn. I nearly made it, but not quite. David smiled: 'Nice opportunity for a demonstration of a controlled mild snatch recovery using the KERR system.'

KERR stands for Kinetic Energy Recovery Rope and involves

109

Panda 4x4 in the quarry section: not as tough as a Land Rover of course, but a lion-hearted little performer all the same.

Into the mire: good practice at getting through mud – or a chance to learn about winching if (when) you get stuck.

hooking a long, heavy nylon rope to the front of the stricken vehicle and on the back of the towing vehicle, starting with a lot of slack between them. Using the Range Rover as a tug, David took off, and as the rope tightened and stretched, the Land Rover was sucked out of the mud with no jolting and drama at all. David made it clear that this was an easy recovery and emphasized the dangers of this system. In a heavy recovery, the rope can easily stretched by 20% or more and as it is rated

at 16 tons it could be hazardous — especially if vehicle fixing points fly off!

We all negotiated the mud-hole in one direction, then tried it the other way round. Gill got stuck then, mud up to the axles. This time recovery was using the Fairey electric winch on the front of the Range Rover. Again, there was strong emphasis on the safety aspects. The rope hook and snatch block were used, secured to the front of the stuck vehicle and

The Series II gets muddier as the day wears on and its crew tackle all the different kinds of terrain the centre has to offer.

the hook returned to the winch for a double line pull. With wheel chocks in place at the front of the Range Rover, winching commenced. We all tried the remote control as David explained the finer points of the technique.

The Land Rover Ninety had a Ramsey electric drum winch fitted. When that got stuck (David purposely flagged it down in the middle of the muddy section) it was used for demonstration of self-recovery using a ground anchor post at the top of the slope in front.

We finished off the morning's activities by using the Ninety's winch to do a mock recovery pulling the Panda up the hillside through a gateway via a snatch block with a 90-degree pull, and setting up a Tirfor hand winch between two vehicles.

Over farewell lunch at the inn, David presented us all with certificates and stickers proclaiming that we had made tracks to the Overlander centre. We certainly had.

Getting to know what your vehicle will do in a friendly and helpful atmosphere makes the course both entertaining and instructive.

Conclusions? The emphasis of the course is on safety and training. At no time does the speed rise above 10mph; vehicle wreckers need not apply. By using your own vehicle you experience situations as you can expect to find them in real life and can be coached in techniques relevant to your particular 4×4.

The sessions are individually tailored to suit pupils and their vehicles. At £75 plus VAT per person plus accommodation, the Overlander school is good value. You come away a better and safer driver, having had a good time learning in good company. Even if you thought you knew it all beforehand. . .

115

8

Joining a club

Four-wheel drivers are a friendly bunch, as you'll find out on your first experience at a gathering of like-minded souls. Meeting, talking and 'doing' with other four-wheel drive enthusiasts is the best way to learn more and enjoy your enthusiasm to the full — the easiest way to do this is to join a club.

There are a wide variety of four-wheel drive clubs throughout the country and whatever the level of your interest it makes great sense to join. The advantages of joining a club are tangible, not just good fun. To start with there's usually somebody who can help you out with problems concerning your vehicle. There's often a spares secretary who has details of where to get the best deals for spare parts. Some clubs even organize discount rates for members. The club will also do much of the hard work concerning green laning. As we have explained in the previous section, green laning is a contentious issue in many parts of the country and getting the permission and Rights of Way organized can be a bit mind-bending for an individual. Many clubs have Rights of Way Officers whose often thankless task is to sort out the problems and build a working relationship with local councils and landowners regarding green lanes. At least that's what they should be doing! Clubs often organize green laning expeditions where a group go off together for the day; that's the best way to enjoy your four-wheel drive, isn't it?

Obviously the club meetings are the most important. It's a good idea to go along to one of these as a spectator to see what's going on. Typically, a club will arrange for the use of an area of a friendly farmer's land (often a club member!) or a local quarry, and put on a trial and competition safari meeting (see the section on Competitions for details). This is where you can join in, but if you are a little nervous of competing, join a club and offer to help — you'll suddenly gain a whole new group

If you are really serious about off-roading, what better than meeting others who feel the same? Above, Land Rover owners vote to keep the company British; below, the Range Rover Register forgathers.

of friends; volunteers are a blessed bunch. Once you've marshalled at a trial you'll soon see that it is the sort of thing you could get involved with.

Some people quiver at the thought of joining a club because it's just not their kind of scene. That's understandable. The nature of the human being is such that in a group situation it is always possible for rather petty politics to spoil the atmosphere, or perhaps it's the sixth form humour that some people exhibit that puts you off. Don't worry if you feel like that; you're not alone! For the reasons already described, it's *still* worth joining, even if you take a somewhat back-seat role.

WHAT CLUB SHOULD I JOIN?

The four-wheel drive club scene in the UK can be divided into three main groups: the Association of Rover Clubs, the All Wheel Drive Club, and the single marque clubs.

The Association of Rover Clubs is an umbrella title for individual regional clubs. As the name implies, the prime link between all these groups is their enthusiasm — some would say fanaticism — for the Land Rover and Range Rover. If you own one or other of these cars and consider it to be the one and only four-wheel drive, then we strongly suggest you join your nearest club. A lot of people will agree with you. Not all the ARC-affiliated clubs restrict membership to Land Rover and Range Rover owners; a number of them open their doors to other marques. The best advice is to ask if you can join if you own, say, a Suzuki, and see what answer you get. If it's a rude one then they were obviously not the group for you anyway! The ARC is a well organized body. It tries to have close links with Land Rover Limited and indeed receives some support from the factory. You really should join if you have an old Land Rover as the ARC are the people who know the best sources of spare parts. The ARC produces an excellent yearbook, which is worth the joining fee alone; it is full of information and adverts from specialists concerned with Land Rovers and Range Rovers.

If you look through the list that is included at the end of this section you should find a club near you. If there isn't one, contact the ARC direct; you could always start one with their help.

The All Wheel Drive Club describe themselves well in their title. Although it's still a club in the amateur sense, a lot of what they do is both commercial and very professional. This is the club to join no matter what vehicle you drive — even if you don't own a four-wheel drive. Primarily the AWDC runs a superb series of competitions around the country. Often criticized for being rather southern-based, the club is aware of this and does try to move its activities around, but it is true that if you are in the South of England the AWDC will suit you very well indeed. The

AWDC has a growing band of helpers who marshal at events, but they are always looking for more, and their competitions, especially the safaris, are undoubtedly some of the most exciting in the country. Marshal at one of these and you really enjoy the spectacle of four-wheel driving. The AWDC produces a quality magazine, *All Wheel Driver*. It has been criticized for having rather too much 'schoolboy humour', but then that might appeal to some of you. The production quality of the magazine provides convincing evidence that all funds are poured back into the club and the AWDC has a policy that none of their prizes will be financial; lots of trophies, but no money. The AWDC's commercialism is directed to help the club member and they always have a club shop at the bigger events. They also have a Foreign Events organizer who, as the title suggests, organizes parties to Europe to see and compete in foreign meetings, principally in France, where there is a strong four-wheel drive following.

Single marque clubs are really a response to the recent growth in the four-wheel drive market in the UK. The Rhino Club is the prime example. The rhino is the emblem of the little Suzuki off-roaders, the popularity of which has been recognized by the British importers, who run the club and give it an 'official' stamp. A number of gatherings are

A chance to compare notes. If you think you are a fanatic, wait till you meet some of the guys in the clubs...

Club membership is a particularly good idea if you have a vehicle rare in the UK, like this Jeep, as it will help you with advice and spares.

organized and as might be expected they are very professionally run. The atmosphere is very relaxed and as a lot of first-time four-wheel drivers seem to be buying these Suzukis, there are always a number of newcomers at these meetings.

Last, but most certainly not least, are the 'other clubs'. That may be a rather dismissive way of describing the clubs that exist solely for the fun of off-roading. These clubs are not concerned with any particular make of vehicle, nor are they solely concerned with competition. They are regional clubs, often quite small (which is no bad thing) and their prime objective is to promote social gatherings for off-roaders. The green laning parties we have talked about earlier are a good example.

That just about sums up the UK club scene and all that's left is to list the names and addresses of the secretaries. (The list was correct at time of going to press, but of course clubs appoint new officers, so don't be surprised if you write to one of the addresses here and then receive a reply from someone else!). Remember that clubs are often run on a shoe-string, so enclose a stamped and addressed envelope when you write. You can keep up to date with the UK club scene in *Off Road and 4 Wheel Drive* magazine, which has a Club Round-Up page each month.

WHO TO CONTACT

ASSOCIATION OF ROVER CLUBS (Hon. Secretary)
G.R. Day, 10 Highfield Road, Bagslate, Rochdale, OL11 5RZ.
Telephone: Rochdale (0706) 30200

OVERSEAS LIAISON OFFICER (UK contact for overseas Rover Clubs)
Bill King, 223 Chartridge Lane, Chesham, Bucks, HP5 2SF.
Telephone: (0494) 783809

ANGLIAN ROVER OWNERS CLUB LTD
Andrew J. Flanders, 3 Mortimer Hill, Tring, Herts, HP23 5JT.
Telephone: (044 282) 2565

BRECKLAND LAND ROVER CLUB LTD
Mike Plummer, 39 Northfields, North Parr, Norwich, Norfolk.
Telephone: (0603) 57841

CORNWALL AND DEVON LAND ROVER CLUB
Mrs Marion Rolstone, 7 The Close, Fairmead Mews, Saltash, Cornwall, PL12 4SJ. Telephone: (075 55) 6726

CUMBRIAN LAND ROVER CLUB
Peter Anstiss, 4 Bluecoat Crescent, Newton-with-Scales, Preston, Lancs, PR4 3TJ. Telephone: (0772) 685735

DORSET LAND ROVER AND RANGE ROVER CLUB
Paul Wells, The Cross, Belchalwell, Blandford, Dorset, DT11 1EG

ESSEX LAND ROVER CLUB
Dave Bygrave, The Knoll, Bygrave Road, Ashwell, Nr Baldock, Herts, SG7 5RH. Telephone: (046 274) 2418

HANTS AND BERKS ROVER OWNERS
Andy Smith, 29 Silverdale Road, Tadley, Nr Basingstoke, Hants, RG26 6JL. Telephone: (07356) 3395

LAND ROVER REGISTER (1947-1951)
Mrs Sally Cooknell, Langford Cottage, School Lane, Ladbroke, Leamington Spa, Warwickshire, CV33 0BX. Telephone: (092681) 2101

LAND ROVER SAFARI OWNERS CLUB
Andy Grew, 7 George Street, Wordsley, Stourbridge, West Midlands, DY8 5YN

LAND ROVER SERIES I CLUB
David Bowyer, East Foldhay, Zeal Monachorum, Crediton, Devon, EX17 6DH. Telephone: (036 33) 666

LAND ROVER SERIES II CLUB
Ross Floyd, 2 Brockley End Cottages, Cleeve, Avon, BS19 4PP

LEICESTERSHIRE LAND ROVER CLUB LTD
John Taylor, Fearn House, 1 Guildford Drive, Wigston Fields, Leicester, LE8 1HG. Telephone: (0533) 740576

LINCOLNSHIRE LAND ROVER CLUB
Rick Wells, Shephards Hut, Horkstow, Barton-on-Humber, South Humberside. Telephone: (065 261) 603

MIDLAND ROVER OWNERS CLUB
Derek Spooner, Bank Cottage, Abbots Morton, Worcester, WR7 4NA

NORTH EASTERN ROVERS CLUB
Mrs June Green, 248 Horsley Road, Barmiston, Washington, Tyne and Wear, NE38 8HP. Telephone: (091) 4169351

NORTH WALES LAND ROVER CLUB
Mrs Pauline Morris, The Filling Station, Pentrefoelas Road, Bylchau, Denbigh, Clwyd, North Wales, LL16 5LS. Telephone: (074 570) 237

PEAK AND DUKERIES LAND ROVER CLUB
Mrs Jenny Williams, 10 Eckington Road, Beighton, Sheffield, S19 6EQ

PENNINE LAND ROVER CLUB
Mrs Ann Whittaker, 121 Brown Lodge Drive, Smithy Bridge, Littleborough, Lancs, 0L15 0ET. Telephone: (0706) 78475

RANGE ROVER REGISTER
Chris Tomley, Cwm Cocken, Bettius, Newtown, Powys, SY16 3LQ. Telephone: (0686) 87430

RED ROSE LAND ROVER CLUB
Mrs Margaret Tate, 22 Bank Hey Lane South, Blackburn, Lancs, BB1 5RQ. Telephone: (0256) 662575

SCOTTISH LAND ROVER OWNERS CLUB
Campbell Deas, 10 Silverburn Drive, Peniculic, Midlothian, EH26 9AQ Telephone: (0968) 76103

SOMERSET AND WILTSHIRE ROVER OWNERS CLUB
Michael Hall, Nightingale Farm, Broome, Swindon, Wiltshire, SN3 1NA. Telephone: (0793) 34372

SOUTHERN ROVERS OWNERS CLUB
Geoff Edwards, 3 Eton Close, Walderslade, Chatham, Kent, ME5 9AT. Telephone: (0634) 684530

STAFFORDSHIRE AND SHROPSHIRE LAND ROVER CLUB

Dennis Jones, 3 Manorford Avenue, West Bromwich, West Midlands, B71 3QJ. Telephone: (021 588) 5892

WYE AND WELSH ROVER OWNERS CLUB

P. Thomas, 1 Bracelands Drive, Christchurch, Coleford, Gloucestershire. Telephone: (0594) 33289

YORKSHIRE ROVER OWNERS CLUB

Mrs Sue Whiteley, 10 Thorncliffe, Kirkburton, Huddersfield, HD8 0UG. Telephone: (0484) 603564.

ALL WHEEL DRIVE CLUB

David Sarfield-Hall, Flat 6, 85 Henley Road, Caversham, Reading, RG4 0DS. Telephone: (0734) 483092

THE AUSTIN GYPSY REGISTER

Mike Gilbert, 8 Thoresby Court, Stem Lane, New Milton, Hants, BH25 5UJ. Telephone: (0425) 618793

BUCHAN OFF-ROAD DRIVERS CLUB

Eddie McConochie, 15 Slains Crescent, Cruden Bay, Peterhead, Aberdeenshire. Telephone: (0779) 813200

THE DEESIDE FOUR WHEEL DRIVE CLUB

Lorraine Allen, c/o Banchory Lodge Hotel, Banchory, Kincardineshire, AB3 3HS. Telephone: (03302) 2625

EAST DEVON OFF-ROAD CLUB

Mrs Wendy Arnold, Birch House, Clayhidon, Cullompton, Devon. Telephone: (0823) 680498

EAST MIDLANDS OFF ROAD CLUB

M. Jaques, Woodstock, Gainsborough Road, Winthorpe, Newark, Notts, NG24 2NN

THE JEEP OWNERS ASSOCIATION

Ron Bean, 1 Chiltern Road, Dunstable, Bedfordshire. Telephone: (0582) 604983

MIDLAND OFF-ROAD CLUB

Charles Deverill, 101 Westley Road, Acocks Green, Birmingham, B27 7UW

THE MILITARY VEHICLE TRUST

Nigel Godfrey, 8 Selbourne Close, Blackwater, Camberley, Surrey. Telephone: (0252) 870215

THE NORTHERN IRELAND FOUR-WHEEL DRIVE CLUB
Ian Henderson, 12 Abbot View, Bowton, Newtownlands, Co. Down, Northern Ireland, BT23 3XT

NORTHERN OFF ROAD CLUB
Margaret Marlow, 2 Moor View, Bingley Road, Menston, Nr Ilkely, West Yorkshire, LS29 6BD

SOUTHERN COUNTIES OFF-ROADERS
Penny Baker, 21 Broadhurst Avenue, Ensbury Park, Bournemouth, Dorset, BH10 6JW. Telephone: (0202) 514111

SUBARU OWNERS CLUB
Steve Eardley, Club Subaru, Subaru (UK) Ltd, Ryder Street, West Bromwich, West Midlands, B70 0EJ. Telephone: (021) 557 6200

SUFFOLK 4-WHEEL DRIVE CLUB
Fred Cutler, Welwyn, Twites Corner, Gt Saxham, Bury St Edmonds, Suffolk. Telephone: (0284) 810167

SUZUKI RHINO CLUB
Ian Catford, Suzuki (GB) Ltd, 46-62 Gatwick Road, Crawley, West Sussex, RH10 2XF

Contemplating the problems of vehicle recovery at the Overlander Off Road Centre.

OFF ROAD DRIVING SCHOOLS

Rough Terrain Training Centre
36 Hinton Road, Woodford Halse, Daventry, Northants.
Telephone: 0327 61886   Mr Clifford

Motor Safari
42 Hoole Road, Hoole, Chester, CH2 3NL.
Telephone: 0244 548849   Peter Morgan

The Overlander Off Road Centre
East Foldhay, Zeal Monachorum, Crediton, Devon, EX17 6DH.
Telephone: 036 33 666   David Bowyer

Ronnie Dale's Off Road Adventure Driving School
Whiteburn, Abbey St. Bathans, Duns, Berwickshire, TD11 3RU.
Telephone: 03614 244/223   Ronnie Dale

Northern Safaris
121 Goodshaw Lane, Goodshaw, Rossendale, Lancashire, BB4 8DJ.
Telephone: 0706 227456   Bill Jones

9

Off-road competition

Ever fancied entering the Paris-Dakar Rally? Flat out in fifth across the sand, correcting the four-wheel drift at 120mph without lifting off, just using just a touch of opposite lock? If that's what you consider you're capable of, stop reading now, we can't help you, Champ. Chump is more like it; most of us have rather more sensible ideas about competition, and if you're reading this, the chances are you own just the vehicle with which to start competing.

If the thought of motorsport worries you a little, or provokes the response 'it's not really for me' or 'that's a rich man's game', then hold on. You're wrong. Four-wheel drive owners have the means to enter one of the most enjoyable branches of motorsport; not only is it enjoyable, it's relatively simple and it won't cost you a fortune.

First of all, let's get things into perspective. The Paris-Dakar-type rallies are the ultimate (as we explain in our special feature elsewhere in the book). But as with all forms of motorsport there's also the grass roots competition, and that's where you come in; RTV trials are just for you. RTV stands for Road Taxed Vehicle, in other words, a normal road car. Just like the one parked outside . . .

There are two distinct forms of off-road motorsport, events that are run against the clock and those that aren't. An RTV trial is not against the clock; this is no foot-to-the-floor speed event where you stand a good chance of rearranging your vehicle's bodywork. An off-road trial tests both the car and the driver's ability and it's the latter that makes all the difference. A good trials driver has excellent co-ordination to ensure exactly the right amount of throttle and inch-perfect positioning. If you enjoy driving off-road, you'll love trialing.

The concept of all off-road trials is the same. At the event site, a series of sections will have been marked out by the Clerk of the Course. These

Motor sport is dangerous, or why you need a roll cage – but don't worry, this need not be you! This is in fact a competitor in an Expert's Trial (sic) getting it all wrong: Road Taxed Vehicle (RTV) trials are a lot less damaging.

You might get a trifle muddy – so don't wear your best clothes.

will consist of short routes between a series of canes (in pairs) known as gates. There will be 10 or 12 of these gates and the competitors will have to drive the section between each of the gates without stopping or touching any of the canes. The position of the canes is not, of course, accidental; they will be at particularly difficult points where the terrain means you have to use all your skill and judgment to get past. The canes are numbered in descending order from, say, 10 to 0. If a driver gets through the first eight pairs of canes but fails at the next gate he will suffer 2 penalty points. Your card is then marked and you move on to the next section. Simple, really; the driver with the lowest score at the end of the day wins. With a bit of practice that could well be you.

There are classes for trialing and the RTV trials are obviously easier than the Experts trials for the specially prepared machines. Some clubs run events that are called RTV non-damaging trials and these would be a good place to start as obviously they are designed to ensure, as far as it is possible, that no damage will be suffered by competing vehicles. They shouldn't really suffer at all; after all, there is no time element involved, you can go as slowly as you want, and indeed you'll need to in places. Only one vehicle is allowed on a section at a time so the only thing you could hit is part of the scenery!

This can definitely be a family occasion and you can both drive — that should cause some good arguments! You can usually enter one vehicle with two drivers, although when one is driving the other must not be in the vehicle; one front passenger is allowed, but not someone who is about to have a go themselves as that would be a little unfair. You have to find the difficult bits for yourself.

Flying off the road. This is one of the purpose-built off-road buggies, distant cousins to a VW, to be seen competing in speed events.

HOW DO YOU ENTER?

So, you're interested and want to know where to start. First of all you must join a club. Obviously events like this need organizing and this is what off-road clubs are for. To run the event the club will have to be registered with the RAC Motor Sports Association and must follow the governing body's rules (listed in the RAC Blue Book, the competition bible for all forms of club motorsport). When you pay your entry fee, you will be asked to sign on, which simply means you agree to a declaration prepared by the RAC MSA which indemnifies the organizers, the club, other club members, the landowner and the RAC MSA against your deciding to sue them if anything untoward happens. Basically it is the legal way of getting you to admit you know what you are letting yourself

The Experts can make it all look so easy, but practice and enthusiasm are the main requirements: modified vehicles like this one are only necessary for the more extreme forms of competition.

in for, and without it events like this would not occur because no-one would be able to take the risk of running them. Part of your entry fee goes towards the cost of limited third party insurance, which is provided by the RAC while you are competing, while it also pays the landowner, the club's expenses and for the trophies you are hoping to win. This is why joining a club is so important. We have detailed elsewhere all the off-road clubs and explained what they do, so we won't repeat ourselves here, except to say that the All Wheel Drive Club often has RTV trials at major events where you can enter by becoming a member for the day. This is a good way to increase their club funds and it allows you to have a go even if you're not sure whether it's really for you.

Check with the organizing club how they accept entries. Many clubs will accept them on the day; to do this you have to arrive at a set time to pay your entry fee and have your vehicle scrutineered. Don't panic, that's not as painful as it sounds. Your vehicle must comply with a list of regulations, which are all common sense really. If you are entering an Association of Rover Clubs RTV trial your vehicle must abide by these rules:

1 All vehicles must comply with *one* of the following:
   a) Windscreen raised, full set of hood sticks and tilt firmly in place, firmly secured to the bodywork; the rear flap only may be open.
   b) Manufacturers' hard top or truck cab with all fastenings secured.

2 Hard tops, truck cabs, tilts and door tops must be in place, the rear flap only may be open.

3 All entrants must produce a current Department of Transport Vehicle Test Certificate (MoT). Where required by law a Vehicle Excise Licence (tax disc) must be carried. Vehicles cannot be entered on trade plates.

4 Vehicles must be entered on their normal road tyres, (*i.e.* those on which they arrived at the event). Range Rovers must use radial tyres.

5 Minimum tyre pressure is 22psi.

6 Seat belts, which need only be fitted if required by law when the vehicle is on the road, must be worn.

7 A navigator may only accompany one driver and no driver may act as navigator for another driver.

8 One passenger/navigator allowed over the age of 14 years.

9 Current membership card of RAC and ARC member club to be shown when signing on.

10 No smoking on sections by vehicle occupants.

11 Vehicles over 95in wheelbase are allowed one reverse (shunt) per section, which can be taken at the driver's discretion after receiving the marshal's permission before coming to an involuntary halt.

12 Vehicles may use original equipment Rover aluminium wheels.

13 Minimum entry for a class is five. Amalgamations will be based on a vehicle's size.

14 Regulations numbered 1 to 12 (inclusive) carry an exclusion penalty.

Regulations from the All Wheel Drive Club are similar (without the direct references to Rover vehicles) but they also ask that a vehicle must be equipped with towing points front and rear. These may take the form of a shackle or shipping ring. The AWDC also allows for auxiliary lights and equipment mounted below the front and rear bumpers to be removed if desired.

Now that's all very simple isn't it? If you're still a little unsure, go along to an event and watch or join in and do a bit of marshalling. You'll see close at hand what happens, but we can stress now that it's a friendly and fun form of motorsport. You are competing against other people, but it's much more a personal challenge of you and your machine against the terrain.

AFTER RTV, WHAT'S NEXT?

When you have watched and competed in your first RTV trial you will doubtless have seen an Experts trial in action. Don't let the name fool

The popular and capable little Suzuki is often seen taking part in RTV trials.

you; really it's just a description used to split the specially built trials vehicles from the RTVs. The Experts have more difficult sections, and have a wider choice of vehicles. Quite simply nearly anything goes here and some of the real enthusiasts actually build their own. Experts trialing is something you could consider after you've done a number of RTV events. There are many people who started in RTVs and now their trusty vehicles have been turned into tow cars to bring the special trials vehicles along to events.

The third form of off-road motorsport is the Competition Safari. This is the speed event where a course of anything up to 8 to 10 miles is marked out and you have to drive it as quickly as possible. Each driver will have to make a number of runs to be classified; this dictates that a certain amount of reliability must be built in — just one single 'glory-or-bust' lap will not do. Obviously the vehicles that enter this are special. It is possible to enter an RTV, but you will have to comply with more regulations, primarily concerned with safety; a roll-over bar must be fitted and a fire extinguisher carried, for example. Most of the top guys build their own very special specials and the All Wheel Drive Club are really the experts when it comes to this form of the sport. It is worth going along to watch an AWDC Competition Safari, it's exciting and exhilarating.

We can't stress too much that you should have a go at RTV trialing. Once you try it, we bet you're hooked . . .

10

What about 4x4 cars?

It may be a rather obvious statement but, unfortunately, it's still sometimes necessary to point it out; four-wheel drive road cars are not true off-roaders. Some four-wheel drive enthusiasts regularly dismiss the 4×4 road car for this reason, but in doing so they are missing the point. Four-wheel drive on-road cars have a lot to offer and are technically interesting, which is why so many off-road enthusiasts are rightly attracted to them.

If the growth in four-wheel drive off-roading has had a rapid rise over the last few years, the equivalent growth of four-wheel drive road cars has been meteoric. In 1982, there were three production four-wheel drive cars available in the UK (one Audi and two Subarus). In 1984 that figure had risen to seven (two Audis and five Subarus), and a mere three years later (October 1987) that figure was up to 32. Instead of just two manufacturers being involved, there are now 11 and the growth is far from finished.

So what has happened? Why all the excitement?

Well, you're to blame, actually. Enthusiasm for off-roading has been such that it has caused many manufacturers to look at the 'mud-plugging' aspect and see if it has any relevance to on-road cars. Subaru engineers must have bowed politely and asked to be excused because they have known the benefits of four-wheel drive road cars for the last decade — but few took them seriously. Until now.

Four-wheel drive as a popular option was really introduced by Audi. Suddenly it was respectable, desirable, not some strange Japanese quirk. If the Germans are interested then perhaps we should take notice, people thought.

The Audi Quattro's introduction in 1980 caused a magnificent stir in the motoring world. People started to take sides; for or against four-wheel drive. The latter are now rather difficult to trace. One of the former was the German engineer Ferdinand Piech, the father of the Quattro. It was technically more advanced than the Subarus, but today the system looks very simple and straightforward. Right from the start Audi hinted, and then officially announced, that they would have a four-wheel drive version of every model in their range. That was a statement openly dismissed by many other manufacturers, notably Ford — a company that now has four-wheel drive versions of the Sierra and the Granada and plans for the Escort and Fiesta.

Today there are an ever increasing number of four-wheel drive on-road cars on the market and they can be divided into three groups: there are the practical 4×4s, which are the closest links to the true off-roader; there are the executive/luxury 4×4s, which offer four-wheel drive as an optional extra and have price tags that make Range Rovers look cheap; and there are the new breed of 4×4 competition racers, cars built for the public simply because companies *need* them to meet their motorsport aspirations.

All three groups have one very interesting characteristic in common; the driver has little to do when selecting four-wheel drive. There might be a lever or a button to press, but even this is being eradicated from many of the new designs; four-wheel drive is being added to a number of vehicles, but the driver is not being consulted. Four-wheel drive is being seen as necessary, almost despite the driver.

That's the main difference between the four-wheel drive on-road vehicles and the driver who has bought this book. You *know* why you want four-wheel drive.

PRACTICAL FOUR-WHEEL DRIVES

It is only right to start this section with Subaru. There was nothing particularly staggering about the early models; the four-wheel drive system was very basic. You simply pulled up a second lever behind the gearshift, which engaged a dog clutch linking the rearward-running prop shaft. The rear prop shaft and drive shafts were already turning. Some readers will recognize that this had a lot in common with the old Land Rover system. On the road, the major drawback was that as there was no centre differential the Subaru was susceptible to transmission wind-up, which could cause problems when the vehicle was used on dry tarmac.

Subaru engineers, or more correctly, the marketing department, saw a potential market for this vehicle. It had saloon car comfort and, in the estate car version, good carrying capacity. It could also traverse mild off-road conditions and was especially useful in poor weather and on the farm. Models were sold to rural doctors, vets and farmers, and the on-

138

Subaru were offering a four-wheel drive option long before most other manufacturers: the basic design of their cars, front-wheel drive with a compact flat-four engine ahead of the front axle, leant itself very well to the adaption.

Larger engines and roomier bodies evolved over the years have made the current Subaru, particularly in estate form, a very useful and versatile car.

Latest Subaru to get the 4WD treatment is their contender in the supermini category, the Justy, with its three-cylinder transverse engine.

road four-wheel drive phenomenon had begun.

A lot has happened since those early days and Subaru have continued to expand their range — they have by far the greatest number of 4×4 models on the British market, ranging from the impressive little supermini, the Justy (this is what the 1980s version of the Mini should have been like), through the latest versions of the Subaru estate, to the high-performing Turbo versions and the strikingly shaped but idiosyncratic XT coupe sports car. They now offer what is described as on-demand 4×4, which underlines what we have already said about the driver having nothing to do about the need for four-wheel drive. In these models with automatic gearboxes, the driver can select '4WD auto' and this is then engaged whenever the driver floors the throttle (it reduces wheelspin), if the brakes are used (to try to prevent skidding), or if the windscreen wipers are switched on (the car assumes that the road must be wet and slippery). Four-wheel drive on a permanent basis can also be selected. Technology has come a long way when you get four-wheel drive by turning on the windscreen wipers, but are the engineers insulting the intelligence of the driver?

The on-road car closest to the four-wheel drive concept of the real off-roader has to be the excellent little Fiat Panda 4×4. This diminutive little

Compact, light and manoeuvrable, the Fiat Panda 4x4 is a more effective off-road performer than you might at first think.

car appears to have a basic 4×4 system (similar to the Subaru's); you simply pull up a lever that gives the impression of being a recalcitrant sink plunger and engage drive to the rear axle. The Panda does, however, solve the problem of how you get the drive from a transverse front-wheel drive engine to the rear axle. The front diff takes its drive from the side of the gearbox at the front of the car and the crownwheel drives not only a set of pinion gears, but also sends the drive to the rear. There is no transfer box for Low ratio, just a first gear that is so low anyway that it is impossible to use it sensibly on the road. With little ground clearance, a skid plate at the front is an essential, but the lightness and manoeuvrability of the Panda 4×4 makes it remarkably effective off-road. The Fiat Panda 4×4 overlaps well between the real off-roaders and the four-wheel drive on-road cars.

EXECUTIVE/LUXURY FOUR-WHEEL DRIVES

While Subaru might have been in the UK on-road four-wheel drive market place the longest, the company which made the greatest impact is undoubtedly Audi. The introduction of the Audi Quattro in 1980 was the single most significant model launch for a decade. It was to have a far more important effect than just being a successful production car – it also shook up the international motorsport world and dominated the world rally scene, setting a trend that other manufacturers took a number of years to match.

The original Audi concept was inspired to a considerable extent by the

4WD supercar: Audi's Quattro was the machine which really established the desirability of all-wheel drive for high performance motoring.

The Quattro was virtually unbeatable in loose-surface rallying until the advent of the mid-engined plastic-bodied racers which brought Group B to an end.

Quattro technology is applied to the new shape 80 and 90 models with refinements like the Torsen centre differential.

impressive off-road qualities of the military Volkswagen Iltis. The interesting technical aspect of this early Quattro was that the splitting of the power did not take place from the side of the gearbox, but from within the gearbox itself. A tiny (about the size of a grapefruit) differential took the drive from the front to the rear diff, a system borrowed straight from the Iltis.

Despite the competition success that was ultimately achieved with the first Audi Quattro, the initial reasons for building it, said Audi, was to make a 'safer, better handling car'. This has been the company's claim ever since and explains not only why a four-wheel drive version of every Audi model is available in the UK, but also why other major manufacturers have followed suit. Those readers with long memories will be shaking their heads now, and rightly so. A British company built a four-wheel drive sporting saloon back in 1967 and it was called a Jensen FF. The initials stand for Ferguson Formula and the system incorporated a central self-locking differential that split the drive front and rear. The system was the basis for a planned four-wheel drive estate car, the R5. That a sceptical British motor industry would not support the small independent manufacturer Ferguson is to its everlasting discredit.

Criticisms of the Audi system were that it split the drive front and rear in equal quantities, 50:50, and that the centre and rear diffs were only lockable manually. This changed in 1987 with the first of a new generation of Audi models, the quattro versions of which (no longer carrying a capital Q in their name) have a Torsen centre diff; this means that the torque can be varied automatically between front and rear wheels. It can range from 25:75 to 75:25 depending on the traction available at the wheels; the driver doesn't have to do anything.

When one company goes whole-heartedly for such a revolutionary idea, it is surprising that its immediate competitors can take so long to follow; Ford took five years to get a quattro competitor on the market, BMW six years and Mercedes-Benz seven.

It was not that any of these companies was incapable of building a four-wheel drive car; Ford, for instance, had a four-wheel drive version of the

Ford's entry into the production 4WD market came with the Sierra XR4x4, V6-powered and no mean performer.

143

Zephyr, similar in concept to the Jensen FF, way back in the 1960s. Nevertheless, their first production four-wheel drive saloon car, the Sierra XR4×4, did not make its debut until 1985.

The Sierra system has an epicyclic gear set at the rear of the gearbox sending drive to the front and rear at the ratio of 34:66. The drive to the rear is direct (it's interesting to remember that Ford were turning a rear-wheel drive car into four-wheel drive whereas the problem facing Audi was that they were starting with a front-wheel drive). Drive to the front in the Sierra passes through a viscous coupling, and there is also a viscous coupling at the rear. These act like limited-slip differentials and mean that the Sierra automatically distributes the power where necessary when traction varies, for example when coming out of a corner. Ford launched the XR4×4 as a sporting saloon and it was soon followed by a four-wheel drive version of the Sierra Estate, then by the all-wheel drive versions of the Granada saloon.

The BMW four-wheel drive saloon, the 325iX, has a system very similar to Ford's, with the epicyclic gear system splitting the torque between front and rear 37:63. It is a very enjoyable car to drive, but no-one would know just by looking at it that it has four-wheel drive and it represents the late-1980s movement where four-wheel drive has become just an option along with such extras as alloy wheels, sun roof, ABS braking and leather seats. There are no levers to pull, buttons to press, lights to flash or garish 4×4 decals down the side of the BMW's bodywork.

COMPETITION RACERS

The most exciting group of four-wheel drive road cars are the models built purely so that manufacturers can enter and succeed in international motorsport. This all goes back to Audi winning the World Rally Championship with the first Quattro. Now, if you want to win in international rallying you have to have four-wheel drive. This led to the development of stunningly quick four-wheel drive specials, but unfortunate incidents involving these vehicles made the international governing body of motorsport ban such Group B supercars in favour of what they then believed to be slower, safer Group A machines. In simple terms, for a vehicle to be eligible for Group B a manufacturer had to build 200 road-going versions for sale to the general public; for Group A the figure is 5,000. That represents a large investment to build what remains a 'homologation special'. In other words, despite the rules saying you must build 5,000, these cars are still primarily an expensive means of building a championship winning rally car.

Lancia lost the most when the Group B ban was enforced as the Delta

Four-wheel drive for the 3-series BMW: the 325iX has the traction needed to make full use of its 171bhp.

Civic Shuttle Real Time 4WD: like VW, Honda make use of a viscous coupling to add rear-wheel drive when the front wheels begin to run out of traction.

Latest version of the Lancia Delta HF with four-wheel drive, the integrale, has flared arches to allow the homologation of the wide wheels needed by the competition version.

S4 was already proving to be an almost unbeatable rallying supercar. So what did the Italian manufacturer do? Simple, it went away and took an established 'family car' design and turned it into a four-wheel drive champion. The Delta hatchback has been with us for a number of years, but not in four-wheel drive form. Despite looking rather ordinary, the Lancia Delta HF 4WD has set new standards in the performance four-wheel drive market. The four-wheel drive system has a free-floating front differential; drive to the rear is through a torque-splitting Ferguson viscous coupling centre diff. At the rear there is a Torsen diff — this 'senses' when one of the rear wheels is slipping and directs more power to the side with the most grip. In situations of hard cornering, therefore, where one wheel may lift and lose traction, the Lancia still has the power to pull it through. It is little surprise that this vehicle dominated the 1987 World Rally Championship. As this is being written, the 1988 season has just begun and for that Lancia has a new model, the Delta HF Integrale — basically the same four-wheel drive set-up but with increased power and other modifications that should see it leading the pack once more. Four-wheel drive is very important to Lancia.

Another hot hatchback very effectively adapted to four-wheel drive is the Mazda 323 Turbo 4x4: like the Quattro and the Delta, it has been successfully rallied too.

VW Golf syncro: slip-sensitive power distribution to give larger reserves of safety in slippery conditions.

146

Toyota Corolla 4WD: transverse twin-cam 16-valve engine and permanent four-wheel drive in a stylish estate car body.

The Mazda 323 Turbo 4×4, while outwardly similar to the Lancia (both are similarly sized hatchbacks with powerful turbocharged engines) it is nevertheless much cruder. The Mazda's 4×4 system is like the original Audi system with a 50:50 torque split and a lockable centre diff. The differences between the two can be felt when driving; they handle quite differently and, without doubt, the Lancia is the better competition car.

In years to come, four-wheel drive will undoubtedly become commonplace for road cars. Companies like Ford are intent on increasing the models in their range available with four-wheel drive, Volkswagen are already experiencing a success in Europe with their syncro system available on Golf and Jetta models, and then there's the Japanese. Toyota debuted their Celica GT Four at the end of 1987, ready to challenge for the World Rally Championship as well as high street sales. In France, Renault's impressive people-carrier, the Espace, is now available with four-wheel drive, and so it goes on. The only cloud on the horizon? There seems to be little on the four-wheel drive front from Britain's own Austin Rover concern.

11

The Paris-Dakar Rally
Building a contender

The Paris-Dakar Rally is quite simply the toughest off-road speed event in the world. It is, without doubt, the ultimate in off-road competition, *the* event that everyone in the sport wants to win, while even more merely dream of entering. Strangely, however, it is only in the last couple of years that the British have begun to take any great interest. Maybe this was because the event was conceived and run by a very *French* Frenchman, the late Thierry Sabine, or maybe because of poor publicity, but whatever the reason, the Paris-Dakar Rally used to be something of an unknown quantity in the UK.

Times are changing. The media is beginning to take a far greater interest, as are British enthusiasts, and more importantly British manufacturers. Not only are the eyes of Britain focused on the event as spectators, the country can now boast top-quality participation.

But what does it take to enter a rally that starts in Paris, travels 9,000 miles and ends on a beach in West Africa some 21 days later? The quick answer is money. To that must be added single-minded enthusiasm and unbending energy instilled in a team of people who know exactly what they are doing. This is not the event for the well-meaning clubman who thinks Paris-Dakar is a kind of All Wheel Drive Club competition safari, only longer. Thankfully, the event is not yet the sole reserve of major manufacturers, although it is heading that way, but even the amateurs who enter are exceedingly professional in outlook and preparation.

One such 'amateur' team entered the 1987 Paris-Dakar Rally and they serve to illustrate what it takes to build a fleet of top off-road machines to cross the wastelands of Africa.

Ted Toleman is a name that will be known to many, for a variety of reasons. You may have seen his car transporters carrying new vehicles around the country; you may know the name as the man who took the

It all looks so simple when you see a rally car at the start of an event. But a lot has happened to get even this far.

Cougar powerboats to the UK Championships every year from 1979 to 1983; motorsport fans will remember the Toleman Formula One Grand Prix team and the dreams of glory that British racing driver Derek Warwick conjured up in the early 1980s. Then there was the 'Blue Riband' transatlantic crossing attempt with Richard Branson in 1985. Ted Toleman has tried his hand at a number of fast, dangerous and exciting exploits. It is not surprising, therefore, that Toleman should be the nucleus around which the first major British Paris-Dakar Rally entry should be formed.

Having decided to enter, where do you start? For Toleman it was a case of 'look, go see'! His right-hand man is four times World Hot Rod Champion Barry Lee, and it was he who went to watch the event, but the experience left them with a problem.

'We wanted to enter, but after watching we soon realized that there was no-one in the UK with the right sort of experience to build the cars. This was not just another rally. This was the business,' explains Lee.

As the event had run for nine years, some people obviously had a great deal of experience and one such person is the enterprising Belgian Luc Janssens; he had entered seven times and finished four, his best position being fourth. It was to Janssens that Ted Toleman and Barry Lee turned.

Janssens runs his own car preparation business in Waterloo, Belgium.

Tony Howard, the third member of the 1987 Toleman team, waves the Union Jack above team leader Ted Toleman before the start.

It's hard to think of this, hidden in the cramped confines of a Belgian garage, as a major Paris-Dakar contender in the making.

Barry Lee (right) talks to the man in charge of building the Toleman Range Rover, Luc Janssens.

152

It's a very secluded garage down a quiet residential cobbled street in a particularly conservative area of the town, only a stone's throw from the famous battlefield. It was here that three Toleman Paris-Dakar machines were built – two Range Rovers and one Land Rover One Ten. Support came from Land Rover Ltd back in Britain and from the spares set-up, Land Rover Parts and Equipment.

Three vehicles represent the minimum a team should run for the Paris-Dakar. Race Car One, driven by Lee and Toleman, was the hare — the quickest of the three, the car with the chance of the best finish. Race Car Two was what some people refer to as a 'paper bag racer'; it was built to a similar specification to Race Car One, but its prime objective was to follow behind as quickly as possible carrying spares and assistance. Luc Janssens was to drive this vehicle. Race Car Three (the Land Rover One Ten) was purely a support service truck, but as service vehicles are not permitted on the Paris-Dakar Rally it had to actually *compete*.

When they originally decide to enter, Toleman and Lee realistically considered this would be a three-year programme. For the first year they would build something of a 'plodder', a vehicle likely to be strong enough to finish the event, but not that quick. Having learnt from the first year, they thought they would then be in good shape to build a real racer for the following year. However, when major sponsor Land Rover Parts and Equipment saw the standard of preparation that was going into the team they supplied them with a far from plodding engine. It was going to be a very quick Range Rover indeed.

The regulations for the Paris-Dakar are, in essence, kept relatively simple. In the car category (trucks and motorcycles also compete) there are three classes; Marathon class is for current two or four-wheel drive vehicles on sale to the general public. Modifications are limited to safety equipment, with some work allowed on suspension and cylinder head replacement. Gearboxes and axle cases cannot be changed during the event. In many respects, the limited amount of modifications allowed makes this a very difficult class in which to produce a vehicle that will even finish the event and it is exceedingly unlikely that this class will ever produce the outright winner. The second class is Improved Production, which more or less equates to international Group A rallying category. Primarily this means that you again have to use a standard production vehicle, but extensive modifications are permitted. It is the third class from which the outright winner is most likely to emerge — Prototype and Buggies. This class allows complete freedom to change the engine, transmission and body. Indeed, you can actually build a vehicle starting from a clean sheet of paper and during the event only the vehicle's bodyshell and cylinder block must remain unchanged. This means, if you can afford it, that you can repair anything, even carry out a complete

The driver concentrates on the driving while the co-driver watches all the other gauges.

rebuild. Ted Toleman's Range Rover was in the Prototype class.

Externally, as you can see from these pictures, it may look like a standard Range Rover, albeit with stickers and fancy wheels and tyres, but that was far from the case. Major sponsors LRPE specified that the vehicle must retain the look of the Range Rover, but underneath was a different matter.

The chassis and the axles remained standard, Janssens was adamant about this: 'Range Rover axles tubes are the best, absolutely the best', he claimed. However, both axle tubes had strengthening plates fitted underneath. Differential casings were protected by rock guards. Both front and rear axles had brackets fitted for the extra shock absorbers, and at the front the 'top hat' at the top of the suspension strut was also strengthened. At the rear, the Range Rover's standard A bracket was done away with and a pair of gas-filled Bilstein shock absorbers were fitted at each wheel (front and rear) using Land Rover One Ten brackets. A further pair of Bilsteins — that made 10 in all — were fitted to the middle of the rear axle. Both front and rear axles had impressively thick straps to hold the axles in place when the Range Rover 'flew' over the sand at speed and gravity would otherwise pull them down.

The engine was very special. Based on the standard Rover V8 3500 unit, it was overbored to 3,907cc and fitted with a balanced and tuftrided crankshaft. The timing was improved with a new Vernier cam gear. The

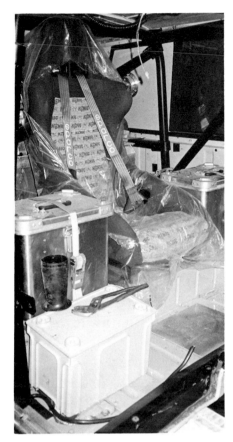

Rather awkwardly, a third seat was fitted to the Toleman Range Rover, left. For most teams, two people per car is enough. Right: the regulations state that the vehicle must have enough fuel for 500 miles. This means that a massive fuel tank has to be fitted amidships.

valve seats of the cylinder heads were recut and the valve spring seats machined to take double springs. The inlet manifold was machined to take a Holley 600 CFM carburettor. After testing in the mud and cold of Essex only weeks before the start, it was decided to swap the Holley for a pair of SU carbs, 1981 vintage. The complicated float arrangement in the Holley was causing fuel starvation when the Range Rover was being thrown around. Electronic fuel injection used on the present day Range Rover Vogues was never considered for the 9,000-mile African marathon simply because it is too complex and would not be easy to repair should it fail in the middle of the desert. The SUs were considered a much safer bet.

The whole unit was blueprinted and run on a dynamometer in Land

155

Paris-Dakar costs a great deal of money and so the sponsors' colours have to be carefully painted on to the bodywork.

Rover's Solihull engineering department before being crated up and sent to Belgium. These modifications provided a very flat torque curve, representing a 12.5% increase on the standard unit. Power was up to 230bhp at 5,000rpm. Some of the other Range Rover prototypes that year had more, but 230bhp was thought to be enough. The compression ratio did cause some concern; it was 9.25:1 and Janssens wanted it lower. The quality of African petrol is extremely poor and competitors on the Paris-Dakar have to buy it as they go along — in *cash*. Local petrol sellers regularly tamper with the fuel before the vehicles arrive and up to 20% of the contents is often replaced with water.

The five-speed gearbox and transfer case were standard, although the team used their own ratios and both boxes had their own independent oil coolers. Cooling in the desert is obviously important and the radiator, while being of standard design, was made of aluminium and mounted on the front chassis rail, not the front panel as it is on the road car. This was to ensure that should there be any minor collisions — rally cars have been

156

A standard Rover V8 is over-bored to 3,907cc to give a claimed 230bhp.

known to hit the odd stray cattle — the radiator would not be punctured. The regulations demand that all vehicles carry at least 5 litres of fresh water, ostensibly for the crew, but as Janssens explained, 'it is often more important for your car to have a drink'.

Standard Range Rover wheels were considered strong enough for the rougher sections of the route through Algiers, but lighter composite alloy wheels were ready for the smoother sandy sections. The tyres were far from standard, being Kevlar-sidewalled Bridgestone 700 R16s. These are extremely strong, and tubed for easy repair in case they are punctured after a team has run out of spares.

The silhouette of the vehicle looked like a Range Rover, but the body itself was made not from aluminium but Kevlar. The side windows were Perspex, but the regulations demand that the front screen remained a standard laminated product.

Inside the vehicle a comprehensive roll-over cage was fitted surrounding the three seats. Three? Yes, the Toleman Race Car One was unusual in that it had a third seat. At the time this was thought by some to be unnecessary; a driver and navigator should suffice, anyone else would be just added weight. Originally, the team claimed that the third seat was for an onboard mechanic/navigator who could speak French, but last-minute driver changes saw journalist Tony Howard in

Two spare wheels are carried to cope with the exceptionally tough surfaces over which competitors have to drive.

One of the Toleman back-up vehicles was this Land Rover One Ten equipped with Range Rover suspension.

For 1988, the Toleman team tried again, this time taking the four-wheel drive Metro 6R4 as their basis, following the example of Peugeot's 205 T16. Extensively modified from its rally car origins and, again, Rover V8-powered, the little beast was unfortunately no more successful than the previous year's effort.

that position. Tony was a good choice, having competed on three previous Paris-Dakars. Behind the third seat was the massive competition bag fuel tank (the regulations state that every vehicle must carry enough fuel for it to travel 500 miles).

And that, in very simple terms, is what it takes to build a Paris-Dakar prototype. The Toleman team were working on a budget of around £250,000. If that sounds like a lot of money, consider that the French works Peugeot Talbot Sport team had three 205 T16s plus aerial assistance in the 1987 Paris-Dakar and spent a reputed £3 million. They were rewarded with Ari Vatanen taking first place, but money cannot always buy you success, it can sometimes get you into trouble.

The Toleman 1987 Paris-Dakar attempt ended in disaster, the team seeming to be jinxed from the start. A wheel fell off before they even reached Africa and they were lucky to escape serious injury. Faith in those standard, relatively unmodified axle components quickly disappeared when they both broke, front and rear, on Race Car One. This car also experienced a horrendous roll before finally it was forced to retire. Then, as if that wasn't enough, a currency misunderstanding caused two team members to spend some uncomfortable nights in an Algerian jail.

Yes, the Paris-Dakar is tough!

12

Africar
Breaking the mould

When you take on the entire four-wheel drive industry single-handed you can expect a struggle. When you turn all the accepted practices of automotive design and manufacture upside down you can expect to hear howls of derision and disbelief. Tony Howarth has heard and struggled. As this is being written, in the autumn of 1987, it is still uncertain whether the struggle has been a complete *commercial* success. But whatever happens, Africar is an extraordinary story, Tony Howarth an extraordinary man, and the vehicle he created a superb example of what makes four-wheel drive so fascinating.

The Africar story can be traced back to 1959 and a round-Africa drive by two Cambridge graduates. Tony Howarth and Peter Turner took a Land Rover Series II on a 40,000-mile journey, visiting 32 of the 40 countries then on the Continent. As Howarth recalls, it was an eventful journey:

'Even in 1959, our Land Rover showed little sign of its 10 years of development (the first Land Rover production model was debuted in 1948). It was entirely unsuited for the African roads. We broke axles, springs, shock absorbers, gearboxes, clutches and door handles. Items that you would expect to break on rough roads with a vehicle sprung like a 19th century cart. But then that was the problem — Newton's laws of motion hold even for 4×4s.'

The journey led Howarth to consider what would constitute the criteria for a vehicle for Africa. Now, this was not some righteous crusade to provide something for the needy in the Third World, this was a trained engineer considering a problem. Howarth happened to be in Africa at the time, but that was almost incidental; with hindsight one can see that he was looking for a completely new concept for the design of an off-road vehicle.

Nothing if not unconventional: this is the monocoque chassis of the first production Africar under construction. Made of marine ply, it looks like no other four-wheel drive in the world.

Three years after his first trip, Howarth drove another African marathon, this time *only* 27,000 miles, and this time in a new family saloon, the recently announced front-wheel drive Austin 1100. He completed the trip and the first embryonic ideas of Africar began.

From there, the story can be brought right up to the early 1980s, to the position where Howarth decided to give up his career as a top class photographer and film maker and instead make three prototype Africars for a special test drive. For a man whose two African trips had totalled 67,000 miles, the test drive had to be impressive. It was. Three Africar prototypes were driven from the Arctic Circle to the Equator; 20,000 miles across vastly different terrain, temperatures and tracks.

'When we came to designing the Africar, it was a whole new ball game. We were looking for 12.5in of ground clearance and 14in individual wheel movement.' Howarth will pause after these figures to let them sink in; both are far greater than on any other present production vehicle. 'I had to give in on the wheel movement and settle for 12in.' That's no apology, that's an impressive fact.

The problem with these parameters is that they would not function with any established suspension design. You could not feasibly force a MacPherson strut to allow a wheel to move that far unless you went through a separate — and complicated — leverage link. The Africar was going to be simple in concept, as are all the best designs. Howarth's answer was to take the unusual step of looking at the French manufacturer Citroen and use leading and trailing arms coupled with Hydragas suspension units. 'I don't think I would have thought of that suspension set-up if it hadn't been done before. A leading arm is a nasty structure, it's not something that an engineer would really want to build.'

The body and chassis of the Africar are not something that an automotive engineer would think of building; they are made of wood. Plywood saturated with epoxy resins is used in the marine industry and indeed Howarth decided on the material after considering a catamaran design for long-distance sailing. The internal sills are filled with structural foam and a steel and aluminium reinforcing laminate is used where required. There are separate subframes and a roll-over bar made from steel.

The first of these prototypes was on the road in September 1983, powered by a Citroen Visa 650cc engine. This was a four-door saloon Africar; there followed a two-door pickup and a six-wheeler. The team for the Arctic-Equator trial run was complete.

Tony Howarth watches over work on one of the first prototype Africars at his Lancaster headquarters.

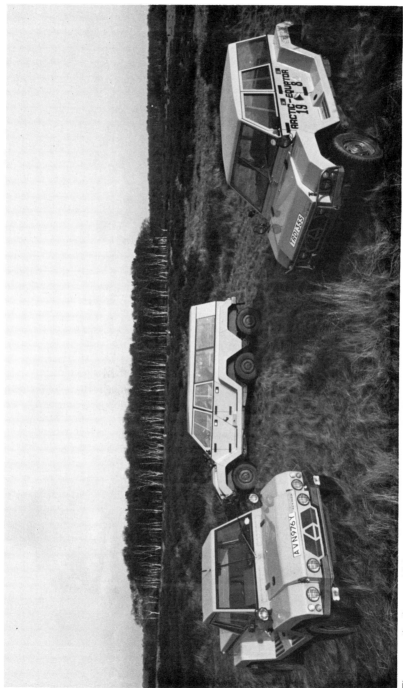

These are the three vehicles that made the trek from the Arctic to the Equator; the four-wheeled saloon, the four-wheeled pick-up and the six-wheeled station wagon.

As if the journey itself wasn't awesome enough, the night before they left for Scandinavia, Howarth decided to rip out the four-wheel drive systems and run all vehicles as front-wheel drive only; a strange vibration through the prop shaft could not be cured. 'At about 2 o'clock in the morning I finally had to give in. We took the whole bloody lot out. It took about 4 hours. There was nothing else to do.'

Hardly the best start, but nevertheless all three vehicles made it, as some of you may well have seen in the TV film made for Channel 4, *Africar — The Development of a car for Africa*. The television company had shown their faith in the project at the start. When Howarth returned, however, things were not as he expected. It had been a tremendously successful trip in terms of all the vehicles performing perfectly through some of the most difficult terrain (Howarth takes care to tell you that their only problems were with the Citroen gearboxes — and he always planned to build his own on the production versions), but despite this, when they arrived back in the UK no-one seemed very interested in the project as he recalls ruefully:

'We returned to a situation that I really didn't expect. I came back seriously thinking that to have built prototype vehicles that weren't put together from bits of old Mini or Ford Escort, and to have got them, still immaculate, to Nairobi would have meant bankers and everybody else would see that we were very, very serious. But within the first two weeks of our return I had a "no, no, no" from everyone. I found myself bust,

The man himself, Tony Howarth, and the three prototypes sitting proudly at the Equator.

166

Any work that was necessary on the vehicles had to be completed by the team, with the equipment they carried, often in the most awkward of conditions.

flat on my face.'

Even the film didn't help because Howarth needed money to edit it all together, and money was now something they did not have. Ask Tony Howarth what it had cost to get the project to the point where he was 'bust, flat on my face' and he says the figure is 'less than a million, around £700,000'. The break came when Channel 4 decided to fund the production costs of the film. That led to the Lancaster Development Corporation offering a certain amount of money and a large disused warehouse. People at last began to sit up and take notice. Africar became more than just a dream and a long-distance driving stunt. The project was underway.

But there was still a momentous step to be taken. Having a completely new train of thought regarding the suspension and body design was not enough for Tony Howarth; he was also intent on designing and building his own engine and gearbox! As you would expect, the engine has many features unique to the automotive industry, although the principle has been used before in aircraft. It is a twin-crankshaft, opposed-piston, air-cooled, two-stroke. A three-cylinder unit, therefore, would have six pistons (two per cylinder). It has a Rootes-type supercharger and will be built in both petrol and diesel versions. Transmission is by a manual four-speed gearbox with a two or three-ratio transfer box. The unit has been designed by Howarth with the ideas drawn and developed by Bill Bonner, an engineer experienced in both aircraft and high-powered motorsport power units.

Building your own engine is obviously a big gamble, but it reflects Howarth's unflinching belief that there isn't a proprietary unit that will fulfil the needs of the Africar. If anything will ultimately destroy this

Through every kind of terrain and climate, from the snows of the Arctic Circle to the shifting sands of the Sahara and the mud of the African forest, the three prototypes triumphantly demonstrated their capabilities – truly a proving run worthy of the name.

project it will probably be this adventurous approach to the engine. It's possible to build a 'one-off' unit that works, but quite another to be able to supply engines and service back-up to the four corners of the world. Part of that problem, however, is potentially solved by the Africar System concept. This means that any country wishing to have Africars would have to set up and fund their own manufacturing plant. Africar International would control all manufacturing and management rights, but this company does not 'belong' to anyone as it is part of a foundation. It grants the right to organizations to form a company to be set up in, for example, Kenya called Africar Kenya. They would raise the finance to build Africars.

Pipe-dream of an eccentric man? That's certainly the view many people have held about Tony Howarth. The point that is completely missed is that there only needs to be *one* Africar up and running in production guise for it to justifiably be claimed a sucess. The world of four-wheel drive needs Africar, it needs the great gusts of fresh air that he is blowing on to a complacent industry. Too many four-wheel drive products are a compromise to manufacturing pressures, economic constraints or just the narrow-minded viewpoint of designers who will not understand that the real off-roader is not built for the ordinary road. It is built to go where there are no roads, only rough tracks, deep glutinous mud, jarring component-breaking rocks, silky all-enveloping sand, freezing brittle snow — it should be designed to go anywhere. Whether Africar becomes a commercial success is irrelevant to anyone who understands and loves the industry of four-wheel drive. The off-road market suffers from having the least amount of research and development of any section of the motor industry. It is absurd that new four-wheel drive off-road machines should still be turned out from production plants with archaic cart springs as their means of suspension. In a world where the motor industry is producing Hi-Tech developments like computer-controlled suspension and four-wheel steering, we four-wheel drivers deserve better.

A good off-roader should accept no boundaries. Nor should the designer.

13

Expeditions
Knowing no boundaries

They don't really need to prove the point, but they often do. Four-wheel drives will go where no other wheeled machine will even venture; they'll even go to places that most level-headed mountain goats only dream about. The stories have become legendary. They are what make off-road four-wheel driving so different from all other forms of motoring; and they are what make four-wheel drivers so different from the rest.

It would need a book in itself to record the many adventures that have been completed around the world with four-wheel drive vehicles. Our space is rather more limited and so we will restrict ourselves to three very different adventures: one, the Trans-American journey that established the pedigree of the Range Rover right from the start; two, the Camel Trophy, rightly described as the last great adventure; and *L'Hannibal* Trail, an adventure, French style, across the Alps — and one in which *you* could be involved.

BRITISH TRANS-AMERICAN EXPEDITION

As we have explained elsewhere in this book, the Range Rover remains the king of all mass-produced four-wheel drives. 'Off the shelf' there is still no other mass-produced vehicle to beat it off the road, and it's been like that from the very start when it was chosen as the ideal vehicle for the 1971-72 British Trans-American Expedition, better known as the Darien Gap crossing.

The idea of the expedition was to drive a pair of Range Rovers from Alaska to Cape Horn — a journey of 18,000 miles from the extreme north of North America to the extreme south of South America, and right in the middle was the Darien Gap. This was an area of jungle and swamp that had never been crossed by a motorized wheeled vehicle like the Range Rover, and as the latter had just been launched as a 'go-anywhere' machine, what better publicity could be asked for?

It was probably because the word 'British' was in the title that the major problem came from the weather! The route down from Alaska was easy because most of the way was hard road. The timing of the whole expedition had been done so that they arrived at the Darien Gap during the dry season.

Unfortunately, the tropical rains were late that year and the military team, led by Major John Blashford-Snell, were forced to drive through when the terrain was at its most difficult.

It can be argued that the Range Rovers were actually beaten by the infamous Gap. That would be unkind, but they were certainly very nearly defeated. The Range Rovers ran on very large, fat, tyres designed for crossing swamps. The large payload on each vehicle as it battled through the swamp must have contributed to the inevitable; something broke. The first problem was the rear differential in one vehicle which, as if that wasn't enough, was compounded by the failure of the second vehicle's diff when it attempted a towing rescue mission. Even new parts, flown out from England, did not solve the problem; the new differentials threatened to break almost immediately. Finally, it was decided to lighten the Range Rovers considerably and have all supplies ferried to the team by helicopter. The expedition spent a phenomenal 99 days in the jungle, at times merely inching their way along with the aid of lightweight ground ladders. Slow it might have been, but they made it, a once-in-a-lifetime journey.

It established the pedigree of the Range Rover, not as a specialist machine built for professionals, but as a mass-produced machine available to the public; ultimate off-roading for all.

THE CAMEL TROPHY

Imagine, if you can, sitting inside a giant steam kettle for hours on end. Permanently on the boil, the kettle is bounced and shaken constantly. No rest, no respite. Then it stops, you get out and are handed an axe. In temperatures of 40deg C and with humidity that makes you yearn for the relative cool of your steam kettle, you axe your way through jungle, at times up to your waist in mud.

Your steam kettle is a Land Rover One Ten and you are participating in the Camel Trophy. And you are very lucky.

Each year, hundreds of thousands of applications are made to enter the Camel Trophy. A dozen or so countries are now involved, and two amateur drivers are taken from each country. They are taken to some of the most difficult areas of the world and they then drive for 1,000 miles

Range Rover Turbo D as used for the 1987 Camel Trophy in Madagascar. Special equipment includes the snorkel air intake fitted to permit deep-water wading.

One of the Land Rover One Ten Turbo Diesels used for the 1988 Camel Trophy is seen here in the course of preparation at the Solihull factory.

One of the last great adventures. Men and vehicles are subjected to all kinds of testing circumstance during the event, fighting their way through terrain you would normally dismiss as impassable.

in convoy through land that civilization has never, and probably never will, conquer.

Those who have completed one of the epic journeys explain that the only real way to understand is to compete in the last great adventure.

When the idea was first conceived back in 1980 no-one could have

Without outside assistance, everything likely to be needed for the expedition must be carried by the participating Land Rovers.

realized that it would become an international symbol of the ultimate in off-roading. The first Trophy was a challenge limited to a group of Germans who took to crossing the Trans-Amazonian road in the Amazon Basin in Brazil. Support from R.J. Reynolds, the tobacco company that produces the Camel brand of cigarettes, saw that logically they should use American vehicles and so the group had a fleet of specially prepared CJ Jeeps. From that first journey the vehicles have changed to Land Rovers, Range Rovers, Land Rovers, Range Rover Turbo Ds and now back to Land Rovers. This is a great testament to the British company, because there have been other manufacturers, notably from Germany and Japan, who have wanted their machines to be chosen. The countries along which the Camel train has travelled have been Sumatra, Papua-New Guinea, Zaire, Brazil, Borneo, Australia, Madagascar and, for 1988, Sulawesi in Indonesia.

One of the drivers in the 1987 event was Geordie George Bee and he retains more than just memories; he has a burning desire to do it all again. 'There are times on the Camel when you wonder why you are there, times when you wish you weren't, but it was an experience that I wouldn't have missed for anything.

'It's hard to describe how it felt because the roads, such as they were, are like nothing I'd ever driven on. If you imagine a really difficult trials

175

Fully equipped and in pristine condition before departure, the vehicles are an impressive sight. Roof rack integrated with the roll cage carries jerry cans, sand ladders and spotlights.

Exotic architecture in Sulawesi seen during the 1988 Camel Trophy: this is travel as far removed as it could be from the package holiday.

Scenes from the recce for the 1988 event. River crossings are one of the recurrent problems to be faced by competitors, but breath-taking scenery is one reward for all the struggle.

section with axle-deep mud, 20 yards distance, say, and it takes you a hour to get through using a winch, then you're getting close. The difference is, however, that in Madagascar it wouldn't be 20 yards, it would be 5 kilometres.' And it would be in stifling heat and strength-sapping humidity, hours on end, dragging out the winch cable and suffering over every single yard until perhaps the vehicle may find grip and you drive for 10, maybe 20 yards before it's time to winch again. Sleep comes only with exhaustion and with all the comfort of an upright seat and your head rested on a solid metal A-post.

So it was with a strong mixture of excitement and anticipation that this author stepped from the plane on to the tarmac of Manado airport for the start of the 1988 Camel Trophy; I had been asked to join the British team for their drive through Sulawesi. For Jim Benson and Marc Day this was the climax of many months of training and a rigorous selection process to find the best two off-roaders Britain could offer.

Camel Trophy 1988 was everything I thought it would be, and more. In the searing heat, humidity and monsoon rain conditions the British Land Rover never really missed a beat. A broken front differential was replaced, repaired by the roadside on a mountain track overlooking the sort of palm-lined beaches that you only see on television commercials for chocolate bars. From there, we crossed a mountain along a track that

Preparing to right a toppled Land Rover: competitors must take such mishaps in their stride.

178

hadn't been used since the previous year's dry season – and never by Land Rover – along a gloriously untouched section of coastline, through the mystical area of Torajaland where the paddyfields and roads merge into one.

It was undoubtedly the greatest off-road adventure I've experienced, and the journey reached a fitting climax when the British team was awarded the Team Spirit prize. This goes to the team that best epitomizes the spirit of Camel Trophy.

That's what you get from 1,000 miles of adventure, a tremendous challenge for man and machine. And once again, the machines are not specially designed for the job, they are merely production machines with some modifications. The Land Rover One Ten diesel turbos that are used merely have a number of additional safety equipment items and tooling. A full-length roof rack is fitted with four Bosch spotlights. Four jerry cans are at the rear and four sand ladders are strapped to the side. Additional strengthening comes from a massive roll cage. A raised air intake is fitted to the front screen to allow for very deep river crossings.

The Camel convoy has to be self-contained and the sight of these heavily laden Land Rovers forcing their way through the jungle is one to thrill all enthusiastic off-roaders. The Camel Trophy rightly grips the imagination.

Relatively easy going: there is still the vestige of a track through the luxuriant vegetation here.

179

Discussing a minor mechanical problem and clearing a fallen tree from the track: scenes from the 1988 Camel Trophy event.

L'HANNIBAL TRAIL

It's all very well reading about these adventures, but this is a book for the 'active' four-wheel driver, so what can you do? Well, as we have said above, it is possible to participate on the Camel Trophy, but from the thousands of British application forms only two will make it. If, on the other hand, you like France, there is a very good alternative.

The French have a rather different view about off-roading. To them, it is all about adventure. It was this feeling that led to Thierry Sabine starting the Paris-Dakar Rally and it was the same lover of off-roading who saw the establishment of a motorized side to the French organization of *Grandes Randonneurs*. Literally translated this means 'great ramblers', but that loses a lot of the soul in direct translation. The equivalent in this country would be the Ramblers Association, but there is a huge difference between the two; for a start, in France they actively encourage four-wheel drives to participate. The vehicle side of things is encompassed under the wonderfully wordy title, *Federation Sportive Des Grandes Randonneurs*. This organization runs a number of impressive adventures in which anyone can join. This author has had first-hand experience with one such adventure, *L'Hannibal* — 500 miles among the French and Italian Alps. It was a journey to remember and one that I would certainly do again and have no doubts about recommending to other enthusiastic and adventurous off-roaders.

You need your own vehicle, naturally, and in my case it was a Range Rover Turbo D. An understanding of French is obviously a great help —

especially as the road books that tell you the route are all written in French. It was an extremely friendly four days in the mountains and the common language was really four-wheel drive.

The route is planned in advance and takes you along tracks in the mountains that are not usually open to traffic. You are actually driving where very few people have driven before and that's the fun. Most of the route is fine for any regular four-wheel driver. Some sections are deemed 'technically interesting' by the organizers and these are the difficult bits. But even here help is always on hand in the form of advice and demonstration. If you get stuck you will at least get out again!

Through the Alps on the 1987 Hannibal Trail, one of the off-road adventures still open to the keen four-wheel drive owner in Europe.

The whole journey took four days, areas to camp were also organized, but it was up to each vehicle to carry the necessary equipment and food, etc. In 1987, the fee to participate was approximately £20 per person to join the *Federation Sportive Des Grandes Randonneurs* and £60 per person to enter *L'Hannibal*. Historians among you should note that I don't think the route had any resemblance to the route taken by Hannibal and his elephants, but it doesn't really matter — it's a great name. If you want more information, contact Phillipe Jambert, Federation Sportive Des Grands Randonneurs, B.P. 1457-30017, Nimes, France. They don't just restrict themselves to the Alps in summer; there's an adventure in the Pyrennes in winter in the snow, across Spain in the summer, and through the deserts of Morocco. Quite impressive, eh? Yes, I agree, isn't it time someone organized a similar adventure in the UK?

My abiding memory of the 1987 *L'Hannibal* was the drive up rough, granite tracks to Glacier de Peclet. When we arrived at the top the sign on the ski lift said 3,300 metres. That's about the height that airliners circle around Heathrow during landing procedures. The sun was shining, the air thin and sweet, I was standing on a moving glacier and looking at a dusty Range Rover with the backdrop of mountains, mountains and yet more mountains, and the winding narrow track that had brought me there.

Only four-wheel drive can give you that.

THE 4×4 PERFORMANCE SPECIALISTS

Suzuki SJ410/413 Performance Conversions

Transform the performance of your SJ or Santana. Extractor exhaust manifold and free flow exhaust system provides 16% increase in power, with Stage 1 head power gain jumps to 35% and +40% torque add an HS4 SU carb and power is up by 50%! Suspension mods and ultra robust Bull Bars also available.

Range Rover EFI Turbo Conversion

The ultimate in high performance Range Rovers. Single turbo intercooled conversion produces 250 BHP with 290 lb/ft torque. 0-60 mph in under 9.5 seconds, top speed 115+mph.
Twin and single turbo conversions for carburettor Range Rovers. Optional intercooler.

Land Rover Diesel Turbo Kit

A reliable and cost effective way to increase the power of your diesel Land Rover. Providing up to 40% power increase with negligible loss in fuel consumption.

Suspension Kits

Janspeed manufacture the only recommended rear anti roll bar for the Range Rover and Land Rover. Springs, dampers, wheels and tyres also available.

Nudge Bars

Janspeed Nudge Bars 'the best that money can buy'. Fabricated from high quality tube covered with tough durable plastic coat, supplied with all fitting attachments.

Phone for full details of products or send £2.25 for catalogue and price list.
Janspeed Engineering Ltd.,
Castle Road, Salisbury, Wiltshire
SP1 3SQ. Tel: 0722 21833
All performance/fuel economy figures by Janspeed Engineering.